STUDIES IN COMMUNICATION

General Editor: John Fiske

POPULAR
CULTURE

POPULAR CULTURE

THE METROPOLITAN EXPERIENCE

Iain Chambers

METHUEN   LONDON AND NEW YORK

First published in 1986 by
Methuen & Co. Ltd
11 New Fetter Lane, London EC4P 4EE

Published in the USA by
Methuen & Co.
in association with Methuen, Inc.
29 West 35th Street, New York NY 10001

Typeset by Hope Services, Abingdon
Printed in Great Britain by Richard Clay
(The Chaucer Press), Bungay, Suffolk

British Library Cataloguing in Publication Data

Chambers, Iain
Popular culture.—(Studies
in communication)
1. Great Britain—Popular culture
I. Title   II. Series
306.1   DA589.4

ISBN 0–416–37670–3
ISBN 0–416–37680–0 Pbk

Library of Congress Cataloging-in-Publication Data

Chambers, Iain.
Popular culture.
(Studies in communication)
Bibliography: p.
Includes index.
1. Great Britain—Popular culture—History—20th century.
2. United States—Popular Culture—
History—20th century. 3. Communication.
I. Title.   II. Series.
DA589.C45   1986   973.9   86–8471

ISBN 0–416–37670–3
ISBN 0–416–37680–0 (Pbk.)

CONTENTS

GENERAL EDITOR'S PREFACE

This series of books on different aspects of communication is designed to meet the needs of the growing number of students coming to study this subject for the first time. The authors are experienced teachers or lecturers who are committed to bridging the gap between the huge body of research available to the more advanced student, and what the new student actually needs to get started on his or her studies.

Probably the most characteristic feature of communication is its diversity: it ranges from the mass media and popular culture, through language to individual and social behaviour. But it identifies links and a coherence within this diversity. The series will reflect the structure of its subject. Some books will be general, basic works that seek to establish theories and methods of study applicable to a wide range of material; others will apply these theories and methods to the study of one particular topic. But even these topic–centred books will relate to each other, as well as to the more general ones. One particular topic, such as advertising or news or language, can only be understood as an example of communication when it is related to, and differentiated from, all the other topics that go to make up this diverse subject.

The series, then, has two main aims, both closely connected. The first is to introduce readers to the most important results of contemporary research into communication together with the theories that seek to explain it. The second is to equip them with appropriate methods of study and investigation which they will be able to apply directly to their everyday experience of communication.

If readers can write better essays, produce better projects and pass more exams as a result of reading these books I shall be very satisfied; but if they gain a new insight into how communication shapes and informs our social life, how it articulates and creates our experience of industrial society, then I shall be delighted. Communication is too often taken for granted when it should be taken to pieces.

John Fiske

PREFACE

I have tried in the following pages to present a series of histories based on some of the forces, events and images that have contributed to the making of contemporary popular culture. These histories are neither complete nor synchronized; they sometimes overlap, elsewhere diverge. They remain open. I hope that this 'way of telling' also suggests another 'way of seeing' (John Berger).

ACKNOWLEDGEMENTS

For criticisms, suggestions and encouragement I would like to thank Lidia Curti, Richard Dyer, Simon Frith and my editor, John Fiske.

I would also like to thank Fernando Ferrara, head of the Consiglio della Ricerca Nazionale project 'Lo studio della cultura inglese' based at the Istituto Universitario Orientale, Naples, for providing space and support for part of my research.

I am grateful to Brigid Bell for helping me to clear permission to use many of the illustrations, Carlo Prato for preparing some of the photographs, and, above all, to everybody in the following list who granted me permission to reproduce their work or use visual material in their possession: ACT (International) Limited; Central Office of Information; *City Limits*; Collett Dickenson Pearce Ltd; Crawford Films Ltd; Decca Records Company Ltd for permission to reproduce the Rolling Stones LP cover; Design and Artists Copyright Society Limited; Granada Television; Richard Hamilton; David Hockney; John Howe; Hutchinson Books Limited; *i-D*; Institute of Contemporary Arts; David Johnson; Mike Laye; John Logan/Shadows and Light; London Express News and Feature Services; Peter Osborne; Eduardo Paolozzi; J. R. Partington & Co. Ltd; Steve Pyke; stills from the films 'The Thirty–Nine Steps','First a Girl', 'The Wicked Lady', 'Caravan', 'Waterloo Road', 'Carry On Camping', 'The Ipcress File', courtesy of The Rank

Organisation plc; Derek Ridgers; Raymond Rohauer; Carlo Romano/Ufficio Ricerche e Documentazione sull'Immaginario; Jon Savage; the Stills Library of the British Film Institute; *Sunday Mirror*; Syndication International Ltd; The Photo Source; the Tate Gallery; *The Face*; *Time Out*; United International Pictures; Wrangler. Every effort has been made to contact copyright holders; where this has not been possible an apology to those concerned.

Finally, an earlier version of the Introduction appeared in *OneTwoThreeFour* (Los Angeles, 1985), while some of the material in the section 'The obscured metropolis' first appeared in a different form in the *Australian Journal of Cultural Studies* (1985).

(Peter Osborne)

INTRODUCTION
POPULAR CULTURE,
POPULAR KNOWLEDGE

Let us begin with some public signs; with that urban alphabet where a contemporary sense is expressed.

(Reproduced by courtesy of the Decca Record Company Ltd)

The Rolling Stones, photographed for their second LP on Decca by David Bailey, the trendy young photographer who, working in the vortex of the NOW (the 'photographer as pop hero', in

3

George Melly's phrase), was to be personified two years later by David Hemmings in Michelangelo Antonioni's film *Blow-up*.

The group, their music, the album cover and the photographer stand together on the threshold of what *Time* magazine would later call 'swinging London'.

Another picture, the skinhead: one of those 'sinister clowns' who 'cause terror instead of laughter' (Paz, 1967, 8). This is the bitter side of youth culture. The skin comes from a declining economy, that of the white, manual, working class. The genuine article – 'Made in London' stamped across his forehead – he clings on to what he has: being white and being British. 'He', for although there are skinhead girls, the subculture is premised on male traditions: the physical defence of territory and machismo ('bottle'), the street fights, racist attacks, football hooliganism and 'mindless violence' denounced by the press.

Like their mythical proletarian uniforms (boots, cropped heads, braces and tattoos), the music of the skinheads – 'Oi' – is a declaration of roots: the street sounds of a truculent, white, working class.

What preliminary conclusions can we draw from these two pictures? Are they only about pop music and male subcultures? Part of a superficial world of transitory images and vacuous values, an exercise in 'bad taste' and insolent posturings?

The image is undeniably male – about masculinity and male sexuality, about the construction of a male discourse – but it is also about style and fashion (skinheads, the Rolling Stones); about the boundaries between 'serious' and 'pop' culture, most appropriately focused in the medium of photography and film (David Bailey, Michelangelo Antonioni); about the projections of the mass media ('swinging London', 'mindless violence'); and about the reproduction of disruption.

Perhaps we could start again; this time taking the Rolling Stones' song 'Under My Thumb' (1966).

Sex and power: the hedonistic prospect of London in the mid-1960s. Over a Latin-style rhythm we are invited not to the private pleasures of the men's club, the guilty entrance to the strip club, or the secluded pleasures of the family bedroom, but to the *public* rites of male sexuality.

This 'black beam' of youth in revolt, and of revolting youth, was, for the moment, largely restricted to a celebration of male desires. But it also led to a breaking up of the 'facile intimacy of sentimental romanticism' in pop music, and meant that 'erotic narcissism', borrowed by the Stones and other British groups from the blues and Afro-American soul music, 'becomes a possibility in English life' (Beckett, 1968).

When the Rolling Stones, five white males from south London, were busily conquering America in the triumphant wake of the Beatles, it was a fitting coincidence that they should be preceded by James Brown when they appeared on US television in *The T.A.M.I. Show* in 1965. James Brown, 'Soul Brother No. 1'. James Brown, black and male.

The 'grain' of James Brown's voice singing 'Out of Sight' – 'the body in the voice as it sings' (Barthes, 1977, 188) – was unmistakably elsewhere, out beyond the accents of London's rhythm and blues and the chirpy beat (Herman's Hermits, Dave Clark Five) of the rest of the British invasion.

But that elsewhere, that other, was also the source of intense attraction. It could hold out an intriguing possibility for imaginative occupations. Voices of the black continent of Afro-

America – James Brown, Mary Wells, Otis Redding, Martha and the Vandellas – were also inspiring London's own white negroes, the mods, to live 'on the pulse of the city' in pursuit of an urban cool (Pete Meaden in Barnes, 1979, 14). A 'holiday from the persistent self' (Carter, 1982, 87).

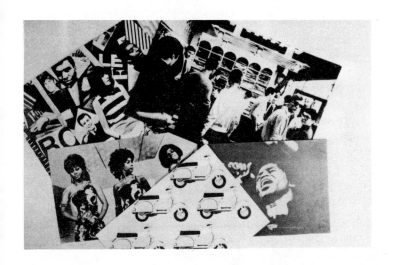

London 1964: the mod. Again a male subculture, but this time he has no interest in being 'British' or being part of the traditional working class; in fact he desires to escape the circumstances that bind him to *that* history. The authenticity he seeks is that of style.

More publicly and dramatically than most, the mods translated the anonymous flux of consumerism into a specific shape, redolent with loaded concerns. Consumerism was turned into the secret language of style, into imposing your presence on the goods, on the present. The mod subculture proceeded to demonstrate how the objects and contexts of commercial popular culture – records, clothes, dance, transport, drugs – could be transformed and moulded by the particular realities of *this* time and *this* place, what the German critic Walter Benjamin once called a 'market-orientated originality'. Through *their* choice and tastes, this particular group of white, working-class teenagers rendered consumption into a precise and imaginative conquest of their circumstances.

The Italian scooter – a rational and economic means of urban transport – is transformed into a mod icon. Set to the rhythms of soul music, it becomes a coded message in mechanized curves and chrome: a cool style that cuts through the grey prospects of everyday life.

Spectacular subcultures, commercial popular culture, America, the triumph of record and television: by the 1960s these were all uniting to announce the death of an aesthetics based on the stable referents of the 'authentic', the 'unique', the 'irreplaceable'.

Such a crisis in values, apparently induced by the glittering marriage of commerce and Americanization, has persistently occupied institutional comment and concerned opinion in the present century. It is a crisis that has proved to be highly contagious. The official universe of culture has suffered some notable defectors, most conspicuously from the visual arts.

Hollywood, Detroit, and Madison Avenue were, in terms of our interests, producing the best popular culture. Thus expendable art was proposed as no less serious than permanent art; an aesthetics of expendability (the word was, I think, introduced by Banham) aggressively countered idealist and absolutist art theories. (Alloway, 1966, 32)

With the rise of Pop Art in the 1950s, the distinctions between advertising, design and painting become increasingly blurred. Demonstrating the attraction and immediate appeal of everyday popular culture, Pop Art produced a timely and ironic statement on the conservative hierarchies of the Art Game, on European High Culture, on the trenchant values of the old continent stubbornly refusing the shiny tomorrow of the New World.

Pop Art employed the despised, more frequently simply ignored, commercial iconography of popular experience: Elvis Presley, beer cans, comics, Coca-Cola bottles, adverts.

8

Eduardo Paolozzi, **I was a Rich Man's Plaything**
(Tate Gallery, London)

Reproduced under the rubric of Art, these objects were re-signified, put between quotation marks. They were no longer merely items of everyday consumption, but sanctified artefacts, centres of the concentrated gaze, of the art discourse.

Whether the motives were to recuperate these objects for Art or to disrupt it altogether becomes secondary. For whatever reasons, Pop Art remained a cool, ironic exercise in definition confusion that left in its wake a tension that could no longer be ignored. The immediacy of popular icons liquidates Art History. A Warhol soup can, the face of Marilyn Monroe, or a comic strip do not require the historical baggage of interpretation used to decide what is art, and what is not. Insisting that the synthetic and 'artificial' forms of industrial life are also 'real', Pop Art revealed an appreciation involving disturbingly profane sentiments that had no need of an institutional guide in order to be enjoyed. The reproduced object hides nothing. It has no secrets, no ulterior meaning. Its 'flatness' is its profoundest statement, 'reminding us that which is obvious matters, that surfaces matter, that the surface is matter' (Hebdige, 1983, 64).

Roy Lichtenstein, **Whaam!** (Tate Gallery, London)

It is this which really galls fine art people about the Pop Arts; printed words are the sacred tablets of their culture; they build libraries, universities and literary supplements to maintain their permanency, while Pop consumers treat them like coke and chewing gum. (Banham, 1963)

If Pop Art took the props of everyday life and turned them into objects of aesthetic attention, urban living has increasingly slipped into the 'society of the spectacle' (Debord, 1970). Caught up in the communication membrane of the metropolis, with your head in front of a cinema, TV, video or computer screen, between the headphones, by the radio, among the record releases and magazines, the realization of your 'self' slips into the construction of an image, a style, a series of theatrical gestures.

Between what is available in the shops, in the market, and the imprint of our desires, it is possible to produce the distinctive and the personalized. Sometimes the result will stand out, disturb and shock the more predictable logic of the everyday. Sometimes it may involve a confusion in sexual as well as consumer codes, in moral as well as sartorial taste.

(Derek Ridgers)   (David Johnson)

The individual *constructs* her- or himself as the object of street art, as a public icon: the body becomes the canvas of changing urban signs. Contemporary art slides into the art of contemporary life, where, in the words of that master of metamorphosis,

11

David Bowie, we can all be 'heroes just for one day' ('Heroes'). We find ourselves selecting and putting together signs of a public identity from the circulating collage of everyday commerce and culture.

On the one hand, the mods, on the other, the more ironic detachment of an Andy Warhol or David Bowie. In *both cases*, it is the *details* of the everyday that matter, that are seized upon and enlarged. The mods' 'furious consumption' (Richard Barnes, 1979) of clothes, music and drugs pushed consumerism to the point of parody. Andy Warhol sent a certain Alan Midgette out to impersonate him on a paid lecture tour of American colleges; the forgery, the reproduction of 'Warhol', was, of course, pure Pop Art.

So we discover that we live in a world where, whether by choice or circumstances, we have all become experts. We confront and use signs – clothes and hair styles, radio and TV programmes, newspapers, cinema, magazines, records – that, circulating in the profane languages of habitual sights and sounds, have no obvious author. And in the end, it is not individual signs, demanding isolated attention, but the resulting connections or 'bricolage' – the style, the fashion, the image – that count.

Official culture, preserved in art galleries, museums, and university courses, demands cultivated tastes and a formally imparted knowledge. It demands moments of attention that are separated from the run of daily life. Popular culture, meanwhile, mobilizes the tactile, the incidental, the transitory, the expendable, the visceral. It does not involve an abstract aesthetic research amongst privileged objects of attention, but invokes mobile orders of sense, taste and desire. Popular culture is not appropriated through the apparatus of contemplation, but, as Walter Benjamin once put it, through 'distracted reception'. The 'public is an examiner, but an absent-minded one' (Benjamin, 1973, 243).

It is for this reason that I have also borrowed from Benjamin the strategy of writing through quotations. The Rolling Stones, swinging London, skinheads, male sexuality, James Brown, the mods, Pop Art, and styles of consumption, do not so much 'verify' what I have to say as refer back to themselves: evocations, not explanations, of what passes through the channels of popular culture.

To attempt to explain these references fully would be to pull them back under the contemplative stare, adopting the authority of the academic mind that seeks to explain an experience that is rarely personal. The vanity of such a presumed knowledge runs against the grain of the popular epistemology I have tried to suggest: an informal knowledge of the everyday, based on the sensory, the immediate, the pleasurable and the concrete.

Popular culture, through its social exercise of forms, tastes and activities flexibly tuned to the present, rejects the narrow access to the cerebral world of official culture. It offers instead a more democratic prospect for appropriating and transforming everyday life. For whatever its actual limits, people live *through* culture, not alongside it. If we wish to appreciate this potential, we must first learn to stare hard at the realities of the contemporary world we all inhabit, intent on that 'wide-eyed presentation of actualities' of which another German critic, Theodor Adorno, once accused Walter Benjamin (Adorno, 1973).

PART ONE
THE OBSCURED
METROPOLIS

1 URBAN TIMES . . .

It is in the city that contemporary popular culture – shopping and video arcades, cinemas, clubs, supermarkets, pubs, and the Saturday afternoon purchase of Saturday night clothes – has its home. Take away this context and present-day British popular culture becomes incomprehensible. But it is not simply the nineteenth-century explosion in urban population that explains the contemporary city and sets it apart from both rural society and previous urban experience. It is industrialism, conspicuously concentrated in the ingression of speed and measured time into everyday life – from the train, tram and telephone to the factory system and the sharp separation of work from leisure – that directs cultural life into new networks, following fresh imperatives.

We will discover, however, that for many observers much in the modern city and in the wake of industrialism has been considered foreign, usually American-inspired, distinctly 'un-British'. These views, this critical and institutional consensus, which has continually attempted to match 'culture' with 'Britishness', deliberately ignore another history. This is a history drawn from the structured and experiential landscapes of everyday life; from its constraints and possibilities, from its textures, from the comfort of its details.

It is this other side of urban life that I propose to look at. It is here, I will argue, that what is peculiar to contemporary popular culture has its home. It is here that both its connection *and* break from the past will be found. And it is here that popular culture's central role in the making of urban culture as a whole is to be appreciated.

View from a train

When one crosses a landscape in an automobile or an express train, the landscape loses in descriptive value, but gains in synthetic value. . . . A modern man registers a hundred times more sensory impressions than an eighteenth-century artist. (Fernand Léger, 1914)

We live in a designed world. (Farr, 1964)

We begin with a view. South London. From the train there are glimpses of Croydon. A genteel suburbia full of those gabled roofs favoured by domestic architects in the 1920s and '30s; many trees.

Near the railway lines inner-city, commercial overspill finds new accommodation, and cheaper rents, in smoke-glassed, air-conditioned offices. Many are empty: 'Space to Let'. Croydon gives way to inner London. There are now few trees.

Low, nineteenth-century housing ('labourers' dwellings' would have been the term) flank the tracks. Then come the concrete acres of Clapham: council tower blocks and housing mazes of recent construction.

For a moment, we see the bold, futuristic silhouette of Battersea

18

Power Station, then the train crosses over the Thames near Westminster to arrive in Victoria.

I have begun with this 'reading' of the city as it allows us to appreciate at a glance how the design of the world most of us inhabit – housing, railways, offices, suburbia, government, industry – is built into the 'very bricks and mortar' (Clarke, 1979) of our daily surroundings. This is the recognizable syntax of urban life. And, like all space, this urban arrangement 'is charged with meaning' (Castells, 1979). It is also charged with power. For the material details of urban life – our houses, the roads we live in, the shops we frequent, the transport we use, the pubs we visit, the places we work at, the advertisements we read in the papers and the streets – suggest many of the structures for our ideas and sentiments. It is this everyday experience that we invariably draw upon, whether in choosing a record or expressing an opinion on the news.

Urban shock

1900: Britain is essentially an urban society. Eleven years later official figures would indicate that 32 of its 40 million inhabitants lived in towns. Such extensive urbanization, then without precedent in either Europe or the United States, was dominated by London. The capital contained 20 per cent of the population of England and Wales. This urban, economic and cultural concentration, aided by geography and by political stability, and reinforced by a national press, was highly significant. In Britain, metropolitan styles have been rapidly assumed as national fashions.

Nineteenth-century British cities, however, were hardly the product of systematic planning. When we picture them they are dominated by sprawling, brick-built factories and warehouses, dirty canals, and row upon row of low, grimy housing: the factory-chimneyed skylines of Manchester; grim, barrack-like, tenement blocks in Glasgow; the teeming life (and diseases: cholera, TB, scarlet fever, syphilis) of London's streets. The earlier Georgian model of geometrical symmetry – squares, circles, crescents and wide, straight roads: Bath, Cheltenham, London's Regent Street – was swamped by the nineteenth-century explosion in population and the brutal rush of the industrial city bursting over the countryside and previous urban patterns. The city was no longer an organic unity, the hub at the centre of a wheel, but an uncontrollable and unseemly growth.

For many, the chaotic assemblage of hastily thrown-up tenements, filthy, undrained streets, smoke-belching factories, and crowds everywhere, represented a breakdown in order, an 'unnatural' society (Dickens, 1911). The city cut into, and separated itself from, nature. It elicited the novel aesthetics of shock, not contemplation. The harmony of the community was replaced by the incommensurable variety of the metropolis. Physical chaos was matched by a sense of cultural disorder. The present-day theme of the city as a place of tragedy, an experience of crisis, was as familiar to the Victorian critic as it is today. And although it was later to be investigated through the invention of two new literary genres – the detective story and science fiction – British writers, with the partial exception of Dickens, found the city streets inscrutable: a metaphorical 'Africa', occasionally explored, usually ignored.

It was as though culture could not hope to survive the rapid mechanisms of city life. Its delicate sentiments would be crushed and lost in the anonymous crowd. In the subsequent outcry against the inhuman conditions of factory life, against slums and urban poverty, English literary and critical writings have also consistently voiced the fear of 'another country', of an alien 'way of life'.

Whistles, horns, sirens and clocks

Central to the sheer physicality of change in the nineteenth-century city was a new sense of time. Time began to be accumulated in collective labour, in machinery and mechanical production, in the factory system. It escaped from the natural clock of day and night and the seasons and became a social construction. It was divided up into sequential units to be measured, defined, fought over, and consumed. This led to a long struggle over whose time it was: over the length of the working day, over establishing the principle of 'over-time', over the workers' rights to the two-day weekend and the yearly paid holiday.

Working-class and trade-union agitation to establish the temporal limits of factory labour gradually gave a new sense to urban working-class life. As industry supplanted more local forms of production, and cities expanded into separate zones for factories and dwellings, the earlier connections between work, the home and local culture became less immediate. The search for pleasure, at least for men, took place outside the factory gates and often increasingly outside the house, in the sphere of leisure, with personal 'free time' spent in the pub, at the dog races, breeding pigeons, tending allotments, and fishing.

There, above all for men (women's domestic drudgery was rarely granted the status of work and therefore their 'leisure' remained more ambiguously defined), was the opportunity to dress up, look 'smart' or 'flash', to translate your imagination into a youth style, into dancing, into 'having a good time', into 'Saturday night'.

(Peter Osborne)

Suburbia

The introduction of new, mechanized rhythms and their disciplined timetables, along with the noise and dirt of rapid economic and urban growth, produced a series of shock waves whose effects went far beyond the initial horror expressed by Victorian writers and critics. Those who could afford to choose where they lived abandoned the city centres to day-time commerce and administration, to philanthropists and sensationalist journalism, to the working classes and the urban poor. London's extensive railway network and underground carried the better-off, and the aspiring better-off (the black-coated army of lower-middle-class clerical workers) away from the 'slimy streets' and 'screaming pavements', from the 'abyss' of Jack London's East End, travelling over and under the 'rookeries', 'dens' and slums to the residential areas that ringed the city. There, in the 'supreme ambivalence' of tree-lined suburbia, citizens of the

22

business world and the professional classes lived in 'a gesture of non-commitment to the city in everything but function' (H. J. Dyos in Cannadine and Reeder, 1982).

So, for the upper and many of the middle classes, the nineteenth-century city became a foreign territory; an alien presence whose 'opaque complexity', then as now, was 'represented by crime' (Williams, 1973). There is a neurotic continuity here that runs from the 'street Arabs' of the 1840s, through the 'gangsters' of the 1860s, the 'un-English' Hooligan of the 1870s, and the Northern 'scuttler' and his 'moll' in the 1890s, to the Hollywood-inspired motor bandits and bag snatchers of the 1930s, the 'spivs' of the 1940s, the 'Americanized' teddy boys of the 1950s, and the 'New York-inspired' black 'muggers' of the 1970s (Pearson, 1983). But these were only lurid symptoms. For it was the city itself that represented a crime against nature. Peopled by a 'new race . . . the city type . . . voluble, excitable, with little ballast, stamina or endurance' (Charles Masterman in Stedman-Jones, 1982, 92), its obscure complexity was ultimately seen as a threat to the 'British way of life'.

Taming the wilderness

The city, therefore, although initially abandoned to the working classes and the urban poor, had eventually to be reconquered, the 'wide wilderness of London' (Dickens, 1911, vol. 2, 279) to be tamed. The publication in the 1840s of a series of government Blue Books had revealed the appalling sanitary conditions in Britain's major towns. This, and subsequent housing, health and education legislation through the course of the century, formed the official framework of what would become the 'civilizing mission' to the poor.

For poverty and urban squalor, at least viewed from the comfortable prospects of a Victorian drawing room, were generally considered to be the result of immorality (the poor were 'philistines' – riddled with atheism, sexual licence and 'the demon drink'), not economic and social forces. Moral rearmament, in the form of religion, the temperance movement,

23

schooling and education, was despatched to the 'Hottentots' in the slums of 'darkest England'. But to be educated for your place in society called for moral discipline rather than disinterested knowledge. It is not surprising that personal accounts of working-class education at the turn of the century often reveal the hollow nature of schooling and its frequent interruption by pupils' strikes, truancy and 'larking about' (Humphries, 1981).

Following the rough justice of the police and the extension of schooling to all, the ground was prepared for an individualistic, 'self-help', 'respectable' British citizenship to grow. The idea of respectability – a medium for moderation in all matters social, sexual and political, an appeal to that subconscious area that the American writer Norman Mailer once called the 'psychic real estate of capitalism' – although often overlooked in pragmatic daily dealings often came to dominate the horizons of many in the working class and the 'lower orders'.

What early planning there had been in the nineteenth-century city had initially been concentrated in monuments to a rapidly expanding market economy: steel-girdered railway termini, Gothic-housed banks and local stock exchanges, extravagant town houses for the rich. But from the mid-century onwards, with the Victorian mission to introduce respectability into the untutored growth of the towns in full swing, and the growth of the political credo of Liberalism (where entrepreneurial energies compromised with patrician responsibilities), towns became the object of social and civic design.

Sewage disposal and the water supply were attended to, parks (the 'lungs of the city') and public libraries were opened, wash houses and swimming baths built, street improvements planned and the streets, often made of blocks of tarred wood, washed and swept each night. Of course, much of this activity, often motivated more by civic pride than social concern, was piecemeal and ineffective; the persistent sources of urban poverty, slum housing and malnutrition – the 'arithmetic of woe' – were rarely eradicated. But what had decisively changed by the end of the century was the fact that the cities – their populations, their conditions, welfare and health – could no longer be abandoned to themselves.

In 1888 London County Council was established. Two years later, with the 1890 Law for the Housing of the Working Classes, local government acquired the authority to build houses. Following the example of the LCC – its housing projects, improvement schemes and architectural solutions – housing increasingly became the central responsibility of local government, and with the 1909 Housing, Town Planning Act a full-blown state concern.

The English home and heritage

Around the question of housing circulate a number of practices – architectural, local and national government, design, domestic life and labour – that in the period 1890–1940 combined to suggest a set of views about the 'English home'. On the physical surfaces of the home in this period it is possible to trace a loaded response to the problems of inhabiting contemporary urban space, and behind that, a reply to industrial society itself. For, surprising as it may seem, such taken-for-granted objects as the garden, the gabled roof and the housing estate can signal crossroads in a national landscape.

By the Edwardian period, the loss of Britain's industrial supremacy to Germany and the United States is partly compensated for by a reflex prejudice against the machine and the rootless flux of city life. The Empire offered a protective barrier against the outside world; and while international rivalry raged abroad, a nationalist view of reality flowered at home. Earlier criticisms of industrial society and the unbalancing effect of city life – individuals adrift in the crowd, without destination or apparent purpose – were now married to the recalled traditions of the land and a common, down-to-earth wisdom of the rural eternal. The empty countryside, depopulated by the harsh rationalities of agricultural and industrial revolution, became a self-evident truth. As an 'imaginary landscape' it functioned as an 'integrating cultural symbol' (Weiner, 1985, 49), to be set against the darkness of the city; a stable referent in a rapidly changing world.[1]

In passing from history to nature, myth acts economically: it abolishes the complexity of human acts . . . it organises a world which is without contradictions . . . a world wide open and wallowing in the evident, it establishes a blissful clarity: things appear to mean something by themselves. (Barthes,1973, 143)

In its blending of the natural and the social (the cottage, the farm, village life), this rustic vision permitted the possibility of stepping outside the competitive turmoil of industrial time into the moral order of 'Englishness', where, beneath open skies, land and blood entwined in a subconscious nationalism and the implicit appeals of race. For if these were the years in which the National Trust was founded it was also the period when Social Darwinism was rife: it was 'survival of the fittest', and the city was a 'jungle' populated by 'slum monkeys'. More explicit racism was of course exercised away from home in the Empire, where its soldiers acquired 'little beyond a contempt for lesser breeds, a love of family discipline and a passion for hot pickles' (Roberts, 1973, 105).[2]

This conservative English dream looked backwards to a

bucolic 'Merrie England' and an organic community situated somewhere between Agincourt and Shakespeare: an idealization of the 'old tyrannies' (Derbyshire, 1983). It turned out to be influential in English socialist thought (Arnold Toynbee, William Morris, the Hammonds, R. H. Tawney), and much literary and social criticism, as well as in the Arts and Crafts Movement and the romantic reaction of the gentry against industrial life.

We drove on and in the early afternoon came to our destination: wrought-iron gates and twin, classical lodges on a village green, an avenue, more gates, open park-land, a turn in the drive; and suddenly a new and secret landscape opened up before us. (Waugh, 1951, 34)

In this 'countryside of the mind' (Weiner, 1985, 6), the issue of housing came to be fused with the 'question of England'. It was not only in the fabulous architecture of Voysey's houses – large sloping roofs, small windows, low ceilings – or the more modest, middle-class language of Unwin and Parker, that the protective national shell of rural life was imitated. It was found everywhere: the 'cottages' on London's Hammersmith Estate (1926), the 'village model' of Port Sunlight on Merseyside and Bournville (1895), the 'garden cities' of Letchford and Welwyn (1920). When the *Daily Mail* launched the idea of the Ideal Home in 1901 it was the cottage that dominated domestic architecture. And if the urban cottage, with its front and back garden, however small, located in a 'hamlet' or 'estate', became the model for domestic architecture in the suburban plans of the building societies and the minds of home owners, it was to be equally central to the newly introduced idea of council housing.[3]

It was not until the 1930s and major slum clearances that the detached house ideal came under siege and modernism, in the form of five- or six-storeyed apartment blocks, mass production building techniques, and clean, simple lines, came to be accepted: Kennet House, Manchester; White City, Hammersmith; Quarry Hill, Leeds, with its wall wardrobes and radio plugs, centralized antenna and laundry, and a waste disposal system that supplied autonomous heating.

Fundamentally, however, the 'English home', with its roots in the comforting stability of the rural ideal, combined against the design of the industrial world and the 'unnatural' city to make anti-modernism a prevalent strand in most official and domestic varieties of British culture. Modernism was to appear elsewhere, in despised popular culture, in the architecture of dream and pleasure palaces: cinemas, dance halls, football stadia, seaside resorts.

Notes

1. During the First World War, Lloyd George promised 'a cottage for all'. And in 1919, with the Russian Revolution resounding around the world and growing discontent at home, the government promised 500,000 new homes in the next three years and began 'building against the revolution' (Lawrence Orbach in Calabi, 1982).

2. Empire and race, with its appeal to working-class territorial rivalry and aggressive masculinity, would later be distilled into the neurotic displays of white ethnicity ('wearing the flag'). When the Empire's gone, your horizons are suddenly narrowed and your own economy is in crisis.

3. In 1934, when many male clerks were earning more than £5 a week, a £24 deposit and 67½d a week for twenty years would get you a £480 house. The interest rate – 4.5 per cent – was very low. By 1939, one third of the nation's housing stock had been constructed after 1918 and the major part was represented by private building. Of the 4,000,000 new homes, 1,100,000 were council built and 2,900,000 privately constructed (Calabi, 1982).

2 . . . AND URBAN PASTIMES

They were the children of the Woolworth Stores and the moving pictures. Their world was at once larger and shallower than that of their parents. They were less English, more cosmopolitan. Mr Smeeth could not understand George and Edna, but a host of youths in New York, Paris and Berlin would have understood them at a glance. Edna's appearance, her grimaces and gestures, were temporarily those of an Americanized Polish Jewess, who, from her mint in Hollywood, had stamped them on these young girls all over the world. George's knowing eye for a machine, his cigarettes and drooping eyelid, his sleek hair, his ties and shoes and suits, the smallest details of his motor-cycling and dancing, his staccato impersonal talk, his huge indifferences, could be matched almost exactly around every corner in any American city or European capital. (Priestley, 1968, 77)

For those living *inside* the irreversible changes of the late nineteenth-century city, cultural conservatism had little relevance. Earlier traces still clung to the streets: the costermongers with their barrows of wares; once-popular amusements such as cock fighting and fairs. But between the pressure of the law and the changed tempi of urban life, they increasingly fell into disuse.

The historian Eric Hobsbawm suggests that the 1840s already 'mark the end of the era when folksong remained the major musical idiom of industrial workers' (Hobsbawm, 1969, 91). Commercial music-making – song sheets and the music hall, later the radio and records – had replaced it.

While the lives of the Victorian upper and middle classes were undoubtedly affected by urban change, particularly in their domestic economy where women were increasingly bound to the home, they remained largely protected from the direct impact of industrialism and the wrenching forces of city life; for the working classes and urban poor this was not the case. It was *their* culture that was forced to change, and often dramatically. It was they, in particular, who most keenly felt the full and novel impact of capitalism, industry and urban living. Unprotected by wealth or property, and sucked in by economic forces and daily needs, these were 'the people' who had to make Britain's towns and cities 'habitable by their own efforts' (Hobsbawm, 1969, 87).

The earlier abandonment of the nineteenth-century city by the upper and more prosperous middle classes, and the subsequent rise of separate institutions in the resulting suburbia, meant that an important segment of urban culture was left to be decisively shaped by working-class taste. It also meant that a public gulf opened up between a subordinate 'popular culture' and the very different forms of public culture – travel, cricket, boating, picnics, theatre-going, not to speak of more domestic pleasures – sought by the leisured classes.

The limited overlap and reciprocity between the lives of the eighteenth-century gentry and plebeian culture at the markets, fêtes, festivals and village rites that had once punctuated the rural and pre-industrial urban calendar had now disappeared. A sharp geographical and social separation between different cultures was literally mapped out along the streets and districts of nineteenth-century urbanization. Official culture was publicly limited to the rhetoric of monuments in the centre of town: the university, the museum, the theatre, the concert hall; otherwise it was reserved for the private space of the Victorian residence or the separate sports and pursuits of leafy suburbia.

Cultures of pleasure

For the writers and critics who defined 'Englishness', the urban tribes increasingly became a race apart, their amusements and pleasures examples of some very 'un-English' behaviour. Even sport was affected. After the defeat of the Old Etonians by Blackburn Olympic in the 1883 FA Cup Final, 'gentlemen' retired from football. Rugby was divided between the amateur Union and the professional League, and boxing disappeared into rowdy halls and tough, back-street gyms. Apart from their popular clientele, these sports had been transformed from exercises in the morality of amateurism into professionally organized, commercial, urban spectacles.

(Peter Osborne)

The same sport came to be socially positioned in diverse ways. While in England, both cricket and rugby conveyed the atmosphere of upper-class, public school pursuits, exported elsewhere they acquired very different connotations, rugby being a popular sport in south Wales, and cricket a mass spectacle in the former British colonies.

The forms of popular leisure that had emerged by the end of the nineteenth century were therefore quite different from those

31

of fifty or sixty years earlier. The establishment of the ten-hour working day in 1847 and the growing practice after the 1860s of leaving Saturday afternoon free for sports were changes that initially remained carefully tied to the self-righteous paraphernalia of Victorian respectability. Free time was expected to be 'usefully' employed. And the tastes and activities of the 'lower orders' – inflammatory recreation and potential 'rituals of disorder' (Reid, 1982) – were monitored and in several cases curtailed. But the growth of an urban commercial culture of pleasure around drink and song, gambling and professional sport, created a new recreational nexus that frequently existed outside the workplace and paternalistic control. It led to important transgressions. Beyond the immediate reach of the moral economy of religion and respectability there was now a culture that 'never demanded complete sobriety, self-restraint or other personal virtues recommended by working-class political and trade-union leaders or the middle classes' (Storch, 1982, 7).

Where local, village- and street-based customs and entertainment had formed the context of early nineteenth-century popular leisure, fifty years later an imposing industry of music halls, professional sport, seaside resorts and the popular press had taken their place. Local territory and street identities still remained important, even if street gangs like Manchester's Bengal Tigers, Glasgow's Redskins or the all-female Check Skirt Gang from Paddington (the names were often lifted from comics) served more to confirm a pathological view of urban life to the external eye than a sense of community.

If labour, industry and city life had been revolutionized by the 'age of steam', so too had leisure. This was most strikingly illustrated in the publishing empires built on 'poor taste'. The steam-driven printing press churned out song sheets, 'Gothic shockers' (*Varney the Vampire*, *The Black Monk*), boys' comics (*The Gem*, *The Magnet*: the home of Greyfriars and Billy Bunter), the popular novels of Mrs Henry Wood, Rider Haggard and Stanley Weyman, popular journals and newspapers like *Reynolds News*, *Tit-Bits*, the *Daily Mirror*, the *Daily Mail*, and the more rabid chauvinism of popular Toryism: *John Bull* and

Bulldog Drummond, where foreigners were all 'wops', 'dagos', 'frogs', 'niggers' and 'greasers'.

But while steam power undoubtedly revolutionized the transport of messages, it was in the transport of physical bodies that it had its most spectacular effect. By 1850, nearly every major town in Britain was linked by railway. Thirty-five years later there were more than 30,000 miles of track. By the end of the century London boasted fifteen termini. This extensive rail system, along with the introduction of cheap fares and a rise in real wages in the late nineteenth century, encouraged travel and the subsequent shrinkage of Britain. The fastest-growing urban centres were now the seaside resorts: towns 'designed for pleasure' (Walvin, 1978). In the last decades of the century, the August bank holiday saw a flood of trippers taking trains from the northern industrial towns to Morecambe, Southport, Blackpool and Scarborough, while more than half a million left London for the south coast resorts of Brighton, Eastbourne and Hastings, or took steamship rides down the Thames to Herne Bay, Whitstable and Margate.

Over all this fun, and money, hung the shadow of American influence on British tastes and everyday life. Already a favourite target for explaining national woes well before the end of the nineteenth century, it was destined to grow in the twentieth. The evidence stretched from the holiday snap (taken with a Kodak Brownie), the piano in the parlour (a mass-produced American Steinway), and the imitation of the pleasure machinery of Coney Island (roller coasters, pleasure beaches, ferris wheels, extravagant illuminations), to the later 'American vulgarity' in advertising, writing and cinema, and the 'jungle music' of 'negro orgies' (*Daily Mail*) in 'jazz dances' at the Hammersmith Palais de Danse.

Consuming change

With the rise of the nineteenth-century city and urban life styles, it is the visual irruption of advertising into the expanding streetscape and on to the pages of the popular press that most clearly signals a new interplay between commerce, consumption and everyday habits and tastes. Initially, it was the dirt, diseases and epidemics of the city that encouraged an army of quack doctors to promote their wildly exaggerated cures on street hoardings and in handbills and newspapers. But by 1850, with an annual business of £1 million a year increasingly conducted by specialist agencies, advertising was already serving to establish brand names in the Victorian household: Schweppes, Crosse & Blackwell, Lea & Perrins, Nestlé, Frys, Beechams, Hovis, Kelloggs, Oxo, Bovril, Pears, John Players, Ogdens.

Effective advertising depended on the rise of mass-circulation newspapers, and by the 1890s the *Daily Mail* had a circulation of one million, as had *Lloyds Weekly*; *Tit-Bits* had 900,000, and *The Daily Telegraph* more than 300,000. A decade later, advertising had become a 100,000-person industry with an annual turnover of £100 million (Nevett, 1982, 70). Both advertising and the popular press were themselves symptoms of wider economic and social changes, in turn characterized by the rise of large industries and companies producing everyday consumer goods for a national market: foodstuffs, drink, soap, ready-to-wear clothing, footwear, cigarettes. And not only the manufacturers but also the retailers – the newly opened shops and stores such as Boots; Freeman, Hardy & Wills; Burtons – employed advertising to ensure that the goods were bought across *their* counters.

Streets, buses, railway lines, newspapers, magazines and, by 1914, Britain's 4000 cinema screens, provided further advertising space. The streets were filled with signs, with a show of goods, with the spectacle of consumerism, the signs of consuming: 'Good Morning Pears', 'Night Starvation' (Horlicks), 'Bisto Kids'. In the early decades of the present century, Gillette safety razors, Wrigley's chewing gum, women's bras and Sun Maid Californian raisins were all successfully established as habitual items after extensive advertising campaigns.

The late nineteenth-century and early twentieth-century household increasingly consumed prepared foodstuffs (gravy mix, sauces, breakfast cereals) together with canned and frozen food. This expansion of the native diet under the direct impact of 'industry and empire' was particularly felt in the utilitarian eating habits of the urban working class.

At the same time, the advertising that surrounded and promoted shifts in diet and fashion, like the ubiquitous sewing machine with its cut-out patterns and their widespread effect on popular dress, was only a part of the extensive interchange between industry and imagery that promoted not only new consumer patterns but also a colluding suggestion of identities, desires and pleasures, suggesting a new and wider sense of the possibilities of metropolitan life. That this new imagery is eventually lit by urban neon or a flickering screen rather than the rural sun does not necessarily make it any less 'genuine'.

Advertising, as 'the official art of modern capitalist society' (Williams, 1980), is not, of course, fully responsible for these possibilities. It is only concerned with 'channelling desire', persuading us to buy the goods (and perpetuating an environment in which we will continue to buy them). What we do with the slogans and images of such goods, how we use and transform them, what we intend with a particular dress, item of food, hair oil or pair of shoes, is another matter.

I will return to this more open and 'creative' side of consumerism in the next chapter.

War, invasion and irruption

In the present century, the greatest catalysts of change in Britain have been the two World Wars. And in post-war reconstruction the expansive image of America, its industrial power, its culture and its assumed crassness, frequently served to focus the fears of a social and cultural order that felt itself under siege. Whatever was novel, often the result of industrial innovation, organization and design, had to pass through this xenophobic barrier.

Intellectuals and social commentators of often very different political persuasions formed an almost unanimous critical front in their agreement that popular culture should refract a form of 'Englishness': that is, it should be grounded in the local concerns and traditions of the 'community'. This organic view of culture,

35

with its implicit appeal to either a pre-industrial, rural world, or the assumed harmony of the classic working-class community of the late nineteenth century, was increasingly at odds with the cosmopolitan modernism of twentieth-century popular tastes.[1]

While writers bemoaned the 'loss of identity' brought about by the giddy commercial rush of urban culture, the victims were busily discovering new identities. The popular press, advertising, cheap literature, song sheets, music hall, 'kinema', and the gramophone, with sights, sounds and experiences unknown to the village and the crowded squalor of industrial backstreets and slums, offered a purchase on this new culture. It was a culture destined to flourish without the aid or approval of intellectuals and the native traditions they and others were so keen to defend.

It was also inevitable that America, as the most advanced capitalist society in the world ('an image of the future at work', James Walvin), should become for both cultural conservatists and radicals (not necessarily different persons) the summation of all those fears of foreign, urban, commercial forces destroying the English 'way of life'.

George Orwell on English writer James Hadley Chase's *No Orchids for Miss Blandish* (1939):
the career of Mr Chase shows how deep the American influence has already gone. Not only is he himself living a continuous fantasy-life in the Chicago underworld, but he can count on hundreds of thousands of readers who know what is meant by a 'clipshop' or the 'hotsquat', do not have to do mental arithmetic when confronted by 'fifty grand', and understand at sight a sentence like 'Johnny was a rummy and only two jumps ahead of the nut-factory'. Evidently there are great numbers of English people who are partly Americanized in language and, one ought to add, in moral outlook. (Orwell, 1970, vol. 3, 254–5)

If the city was the obvious home of crime, the detective was its privileged literary explorer. But with Britain's most famous gentleman detective, Sherlock Holmes, the 'fogs of Baker Street' are penetrated by a 'passion for definite and exact knowledge'. Crime is removed from the streets and passions of the everyday. It becomes the object of individual logic, not city life; a 'version of pure intelligence penetrating the obscurity which baffled ordinary men' (Williams, 1973, 229).[2] By the 1920s, the tenuous links to urban experience in English detective stories had been almost completely severed by removal to the country house (Lord Peter Wimsey, Hercule Poirot, and the inevitable butler), where, with rare exceptions, there is no gratuitous violence, no evil intelligence, no sex, just bloodless intrigue.

By the end of the 1930s, in popular literature, in pulp magazines like *True Detective* and *Detective Weekly*, in boys' comics like *Hotspur*, *Rover*, and the *Wizard*, and in crime fiction in general, the terse prose of transatlantic actions had replaced the drawing-room mannerisms of the English murder story.[3] English 'remains a class language and that is its fatal defect. The English writer is a gentleman first and a writer second' (Raymond Chandler in Warpole, 1983, 29).

As a cypher of urban living the gap left by the migration of the native detective story to the countryside is filled by the American 'private eye'. He, and his alter-ego, the gangster, encapsulate the masculine drama of the 'man. of the city'. The abstract logic and puzzles of the 'whodunit' was replaced by the physical instinct, frequently survival instinct, of the 'hard-boiled' investigator who in the end does not hand over the guilty to a solid moral and social order but reveals a battered code of individual integrity and an urban realism cynically stripped of false values: the city is corrupt, but it is real. All of which leaves George Orwell to conclude rather gloomily that 'Freud and Machiavelli have reached the outer suburbs' (Orwell, 1970, vol. 3, 260).[4]

The contradictions between a firm grasp of native values and the 'superficiality' of popular American culture are probably most neatly captured in the exposed role of the BBC in those years. Under its Director General, John Reith, the BBC, although often accused of being a purveyor of popular taste, saw itself very much as a bulwark against mass (i.e. 'American') culture. But as a popular medium – in 1931 more than 4½ million radio licences were purchased – it had constantly to confront and negotiate that pressure.

In terms of the mass culture debate, then, the BBC's production staff found themselves in an odd position. Working in a mass medium with explicitly anti-mass cultural principles, they had daily to answer the questions that⁹ other intellectuals avoided. What did it mean to construct a national culture? Who were 'the people'? What did it mean to please the public? (Frith, 1983, 105)

In the end, when the pressure of cheap commercial culture coming from Britain's wartime ally could no longer be resisted, it could only stage a delaying, rearguard action.

. . . a show which had cost the sponsors $12,000 was available to the BBC for £15. Soon Bob Hope and Jack Benny were proving popular with British audiences. But the imports were carefully restricted, being broadcast at 12.30 pm on Sundays rather than in peak evening periods. (Cardiff and Scannell, 1981, 67)

The Second World War and the stationing of American soldiers on British soil finally turned 'mass culture' and the 'spectre of Americanization' into an immediate reality. The filtered movement of American cinema, popular music and 'Yank mags' across the Atlantic in the 1930s was supplemented by the direct impact of gum-chewing American males swigging beer straight from the bottle in the local pub, who had their own radio station (the American Forces Network), their own music ('swing'), their own cigarettes, their own particular presence. Despite the hostility this alien force aroused in the pinched economic and cultural circumstances of war-time Britain – Americans were 'over-paid, over-sexed and over here' – it undoubtedly added concrete shape to a sense of the alternative in British popular culture.[5] This was driven home after the 1940s by the ominous vanguard of youth and the rise, as economic conditions once again permitted a certain 'purchase on style'

(Geoffrey Pearson), of the 'Americanized teenager', rock'n'roll, 'juvenile delinquency', and 'all that jazz'.

Now I was ready to hit the town. I made my way down the stairs and into the brightness of the summer evening. I made my way down Brooke Road to the High Street, where I could catch the number 647 trolley bus to Dalston. I looked swell in my knee-length jacket, thick, crepe-soled shoes, bright yellow tie in the most gigantic knot. I wore nice, well pressed trousers on Saturday night. During the week it would be jeans or denims. (Barnes, 1976, 174)

Notes

1. Not that the idea of 'community' does not continue to be very important in particular circumstances. In Britain, the cultural resilience of West Indian, Pakistani and Indian communities is an obvious example. But the making of these communities among contemporary racial, and racist, pressures is different from the singular resistance of the mining villages, through the bitter strike of 1984, to the threatened reduction of a traditional working-class economy and 'way of life'; a way of life where the interweaving of the long histories of class, culture and community have consistently returned to a stable image of 'manhood' and the dignity of (male) labour for its politics and explanations. These different communities belong to different histories; one to the white, male, British working class; the other to imperialism, third-world poverty, immigration and racism. Their differences can be as important as their points of contact. As many of those involved, permanently unemployed black youth and young women for example, are strictly part of a growing lumpenproletariat of urban 'marginals', they cannot automatically be slipped into the presumed solidarity of the politics and culture of the traditional British labour movement.

2. As a gentleman amateur, Holmes also wrote monographs on such details of detection as cigar ash and secret writing. At this point in the late nineteenth and early twentieth century,

detective fiction is suggestively linked, through the then optimistic prospects of science, to that other new literary genre, science fiction.

3. James Hadley Chase wrote more than eighty thrillers, all set in the USA. Chase, real name René Raymond, was English, and except for a month as a tourist in Florida had never been to the United States. Using American street maps, a slang dictionary and police reports he invented 'America'.

4. I have drawn here on George Orwell's essay 'Raffles and Miss Blandish', first published in 1944. It should be read alongside another Orwellian article, 'Decline of the English Murder' (1946), to get the full flavour of Orwell's antipathy towards the 'Americanization' of British popular culture: where 'domesticity' was being unhinged by the 'anonymous life of the dance halls and the false values of American film'. The essays are in Orwell (1970), volumes 3 and 4 respectively.

5. The social impact of the arrival of US troops in war-time Britain has been graphically recreated in John Schlesinger's film *Yanks* (1979).

3 INSIDE THE PRESENT

. . . that enormous present which is without past or future, memory or planned intention. (Mailer, 1957, 271)

Expanding the consciousness of many (for the sake of consumerism) *does* mean expanding their consciousness. (Mitchell, 1971, 31)

In the 1950s, as tower blocks were raised and relative affluence replaced some of the deprivation of the 1930s, the war, and the immediate post-war years, Britain presented evidence of a new social stability, with full employment, consensus politics, an economic boom and the 'Welfare State'. The expansion in the economy (largely based on the production of domestic consumer goods), and a rise in overall living standards, was publicly contrasted with the pre-war world of poverty, mass unemployment, and rigid social divisions. With rash enthusiasm, the 'age of affluence' was declared.

Youth was . . . a powerful but concealed *metaphor* for social change: the compressed image of a society which had crucially changed in terms of basic life-styles and values – changed in ways calculated to upset the official political framework, but ways *not yet calculable in*

traditional political terms. . . . (Smith, Blackwell and
Immirzi, 1975, 242)

For many, the post-war spending spree, a growing hedonism,
and juvenile disaffiliation had an all-too-obvious explanation.

Working-class youth had entered employment during the biggest economic boom of the twentieth century. They had surplus cash in their pockets and an expanding consumer industry soon discovered it, leading to the birth of the 'teenage' market. But that only sets some of the conditions. It does not explain why particular styles of clothing and music, as opposed to others, 'took off', it does not engage with the sense or the feel of the situation; it only repeats the obvious: culture is constructed from given circumstances. This is true. But what is more significant is how these conditions are experienced and lived out, how they are moulded, shaped, rearranged, translated and modified to meet particular concerns and needs.

It is out of these textures, this flexible dialogue between the given and the possible, that unsuspected developments emerge. These, in their own small ways, transform the way we look at much wider realities.

Local culture, and its street economy of the corner shop, the pub, and back-to-back housing, was increasingly subject to irruption, sometimes dispersal, and, almost without exception, remaking. Britain's bomb-damaged city centres were rebuilt and extensive slum clearance and rehousing programmes undertaken. Private and public capital, local government housing policy and architecture, the arrival of television, and the expansion of the media and entertainment industries, the introduction of shopping centres and supermarkets: all combined to remould the physical, social and symbolic structures of urban life.

Buildings and food

In chapter 1 we saw that the 'jazz style' of modern architecture encountered much resistance in Britain from the 'cottage' ideal of architecture. After the experience of the nineteenth-century urban explosion, the city was considered to be a conspiracy against real needs; it was lived as a drama, a crisis, not as an opportunity to reorganize and launch new projects. The bold intentions of the Crystal Palace, constructed in 1851, proved to be a cul-de-sac for British architecture, an engineering curiosity;

its steel and glass design was eventually followed up elsewhere, on the Continent and in the USA.

Thus modernism, that seamless web of total design that stretches from a wrist-watch to a city, initially only registered in the commercial margins of British townscapes: in the 1930s in Walter Gilbert's Hoover Factory on London's Westway, in the occasional domestic expanses of flat, white surfaces – the Modern House – in the Thames valley (an 'abstract beauty in sunlight before their first winter staining', Esher, 1983, 38), in the Art Deco style of the Odeon cinemas and an occasional department store.

(Mike Laye)

The absence of a native modernist vision on the scale of the French Le Corbusier or the German Bauhaus school lay in a deep uncertainty about the modern relationship between architecture, art, design, craft and manufacture. The origins of this uncertainty lay in the cottage mythology of the English home, subsequently extended into the concept of the garden city, into anti-industrialism and suburbia.

It was not until the 1950s that modernist architecture became fully part of the public domain and debate. The repair and rehabilitation of Britain's major cities after depression and war provided an opportunity for new solutions. It introduced the Corbusian epoch of the 'New Brutalism' on a mass scale: unadorned concrete, exposed pipes, steel and glass, 'streets in the air', and expressways driven through the heart of the city (Birmingham, Newcastle) to permit rapid escape from the new urban cement.

As the '50s dissolved into the '60s and high-rise tower blocks advanced eastwards across south London, together with multi-storeyed car parks, shopping malls and traffic-free precincts, the optimism of post-war public housing authorities slackened. Complaints by tenants of feeling isolated in their 'sky flats', sociologists' warnings about the social dangers of community-less housing estates, the drawbacks of prefabricated building units that were subject to draughts, leaks and high heating costs, and the gas explosion disaster of Ronan Point in 1968, apparently condemned the whole post-war experiment in public urban rehousing.

By the 1970s, a conservative backlash against modernism and its architecture was in full swing. It was conveniently forgotten that the Georgian and Victorian house styles that were often proposed as alternatives to tower blocks and high-density estates were of a kind that had co-existed with giant urban slums and had required high individual incomes (and servants) to make them habitable. The contemporary gentrification and modification of these houses with Terence Conran's Habitat range of understated modern furniture and Laura Ashley's tasteful, traditionalist fabrics is hardly an option open to all.[1]

Both public housing and the property boom of the 1960s (symbolized by the Centre Point tower on the corner of New Oxford Street and Tottenham Court Road) changed Britain's urban skylines. But the heavy slabs of grey concrete, accentuated by their relatively low height, usually lacked the grace,

imagination and vertical integration, encouraged by street-grid co-ordination, of North American skyscrapers.

Constrained by ideology as well as by economics, the British could not emulate the high drama or the glamour that were the great assets of American modernism. Indeed it is the timidity rather than the vulgarity of English 'skyscrapers' that is their most depressing feature. (Esher, 1983, 285)

In the wake of the brave new world spirit of the 1950s and the widespread criticisms of modern, but sometimes paternalistic, sometimes insensitive, architectural solutions that at times seemed to be in sharp contrast to the daily needs and habits of those living in the abstractly conceived houses, streets and neighbourhoods, the 1970s and '80s have revealed a more pragmatic eclecticism. The new town of Milton Keynes, the Barbican project, the redevelopment of Covent Garden, and the realization of the TV-AM studios in Camden Town, represent four very different forms of townscapes, streetscapes, urban living and building. Yet, from Milton Keynes's million square feet of shopping centre, all at ground level with direct car access along its linear front, to the intimacy of Covent Garden's piazza, architecture seems to have refined the former ideals of modernism ('designing the city') into more modest proposals for local,

A window on one type of British home: static shapes, textures, tastes and arrangements. The solid traditions of native domesticity – drawn from some mythical moment in the nineteenth century – are preferred to the possibilities of contemporary design.

working solutions and architectural decoration. In a phrase coined within architecture itself, it has gone 'post-modern'.

Changes in the city were not limited to the physical shape of buildings and public housing. They also involved the gradual making of new sensibilities and changing tastes in the home, design, shopping and food. Over the last 150 years it is not only the city that has changed much of its appearance; there has also occurred a revolution in food and eating habits, in the preparation, presentation and distribution of everyday alimentation. Our diet, even more than our homes or streets, has changed dramatically. Over a very brief period of time our bodies have been subject to a massive intake of processed foods (in particular refined carbohydrates – flour and sugar) and a corresponding reduction in raw fibre intake that has produced a new pathology: diabetes, varicose veins, obesity, coronary thrombosis, constipation. This, in turn, has induced further changes in eating habits. Along with 'real ale', integral foodstuffs – wholemeal bread, brown rice, muesli – re-enter the self-consciously 'healthy' middle-class diet; sugar is abandoned.

Shops, supermarkets and restaurants increasingly support these alimentary alternatives.

So, the range available to the contemporary palate is potentially wider than ever before, stretching from international fast food (Wimpy, McDonalds, Pizza Express) to the widespread discovery of post-Empire culinary tastes (Indian and Chinese cooking) and macrobiotic diets. The resources of the world are not, however, limitless. The range and richness of diet in Britain, as in northern Europe, and the United States, frequently also represents the poverty of diet elsewhere. When third-world agricultures are turned over to the production of cash crops, often for livestock feed for Europe and North America, local malnutrition and famine can be directly connected to the hamburger on our plate and the milk in our cup. Meanwhile, British supermarkets, as marked by class distinctions as any other public institution in British life – the creamy–illuminated Sainsbury delicatessen contrasting sharply with the mountain-high stacked cans of baked beans in Tesco's – offer you the ingredients of a planetary cuisine, from oven-ready pasta to fresh mango, Danish bacon and barbecue sauce.

These rapid changes in diet and buildings are also linked to the reorganization of domestic space and labour following the large-scale introduction of such domestic consumer items as electric fires, fridges, washing machines, improved cookers, Hoovers, the private car (essential for effective supermarket shopping), food blenders, eye-level grills, microwave-ovens. In the relatively brief span of three decades (1950s–1980s), both the shape and contents of public and private space have changed sharply. And although the effects have no doubt been largely limited to the level of our subconscious, it has affected both the structure and feel of our experiences and expectations.

Old tastes, new tastes: signs of social life

Dick Hebdige has brilliantly explored how in literature, social criticism and design circles, amongst the 'taste makers', the controversy that grew up in the 1950s and 1960s around this overall shift in British life styles repeated the perennials: native traditions versus 'foreign invasions'.[2] The object of critical disdain for some was merely modernism altogether. For others it was the threat to the uncluttered rationality of inter-war European modernism (straight lines, white surfaces, no decoration, clean functionalism) represented by the baroque extravagance of 1950s American streamlining and, to a lesser extent, post-war Continental styling. The exaggerated size, shape and finish of American cars – tailfins stolen from a jet(!), *four* headlights, all that chrome – and the sculptured 'Italian line' in office furniture, scooters, espresso machines, coffee bars and interior design, generated a hostile reaction in various quarters in Britain. The Americans were accused of 'debauching themselves in tailfins' (Reyner Banham), and the 'effeminate', under-powered, Italian motor-scooter was compared unfavourably to that 'bestiary of power' (Roland Barthes), the noisy British motor bike and its 'masculine culture of the road' (Dick Hebdige).

This debate, and its references to 'trash' culture and effete mannerisms, carries us, through modernism, America, and the Continent, to the adoption of conspicuous 'foreign' habits in post-war British youth styles.

In male subcultures a foreign influence, an 'Other', frequently of transatlantic inspiration, has been unfailingly present: Teddy boys and their stylistic homage to the American zoot suit and the Hollywood gangster; the mods who drew equally on black American soul music and Continental fashion, crossed James Brown with Milan, then self-consciously 'drifted out at night looking for action with a black man's code to fit the facts' (Mailer, 1957).

These attempts at imposing private obsessions on public places (the 'wild ones', the 'cool ones', the 'faces'), of translating an imagined state into the clothes, music and style of a carefully studied live performance, promised a temporary escape from your time, your circumstances, your history.

The new sensibility – *Baby baby baby where did our love go?* – the new world, submerged so long, invisible, and now arising, slippy, shiny, electric – Super Scuba-man – out of the vinyl deeps. (Wolfe, 1966, 16)

(David Johnson)

(Reproduced by courtesy of the *Sunday Mirror*)

Although the codes were secret, the signs were public and exposed youth culture to moments of orchestrated scandal in the media where the desire for the 'Other', for difference, came to be labelled simply as 'anti-social behaviour'.

An attempt, if you like, to show that what is recognizable in British life need not be bound to 'solid breakfasts and gloomy Sundays, smoky towns and winding roads, green fields and red pillar boxes' (Orwell, 1970, vol. 2, 76).

What was most shocking, for critics of all political persuasions, was that these youth groups adapted their styles from consumer objects, that their cultural insubordination was allied to a consumerism that touched a very un-British hedonism as it 'squandered' its money on extravagant clothing, pop records, scooters, over-priced frothy coffee, motor bikes, drugs, clubs, and attempts to create a perpetual 'weekend'. This slackness in social and sartorial decorum naturally also played upon the fears of a youthful sexuality freed from discipline and constraint (the

Against a greenish drape background a young man plays the saxophone. In front of him a red-headed girl dressed in black is dancing alone, hands behind her head. Her body is transported by music, ecstasy, desire. . . . This is the cover of the 1962 Panther edition of American beat writer Jack Kerouac's The Subterraneans. *For two and sixpence you were promised an 'unashamed look' at 'weird lives' and 'wild loves . . . in a jazz-haunted, desire-tormented world'.*

abolition of National Service in 1960 was considered particularly significant here) seduced by the permissive freedom of 'America'. These developments outraged not only the stiff-lipped middle classes, but also the 'respectable' working class, where masculinity was traditionally endorsed through hard, physical work and an unambiguous toughness, and all this male narcissism, with its attention to the 'look', to the details, to the length of jacket vents, velvet on the collar, and the number of buttons on the sleeves, to fussy hair styles and foppishly pointed shoes, all this dressing up in public, was disturbing.

But while subcultures have largely been exercises in the physical, sexual and sartorial bravado of male street styles, playing with stylized indentities is actually, usually in a much quieter fashion, a central concern for most of us in urban life. Fashion is ambiguous: it is simultaneously about advertising, about marketing, about the fashionable consensus, *and* about our construction of our public selves. For the consumption of everyday goods also involves the consumption of social signs; we construct our identities from 'borrowed ready-mades lifted from the catalogue of urban life' (Del Sapio, forthcoming).

The drama of male subcultural styles can easily divert attention from the more low key, more persuasive projection of styles and fashion that through girls', women's and fashion magazines, television programmes and shops, are part of a larger urban spectacle.[3]

For women, fashion can become a foil for public assertions, and the forbidden iconography of marginal womanhood ('vulgar' cosmetics, skimpy clothing, leather, the 'bold look') can be recycled to produce a challenge to male judgement and a refusal to be sentenced by that gaze (Hebdige, 1982).

When 'girls want to have fun', the female libido in the promiscuous world of goods can upset previous identities, can pose threats to the powers, values and institutions of British manhood. More than this, the concern with the body – both female and male – in fashion, pop music and dance, can lead into ambiguity, an escape from previous roles and an assumption of new ones.

54

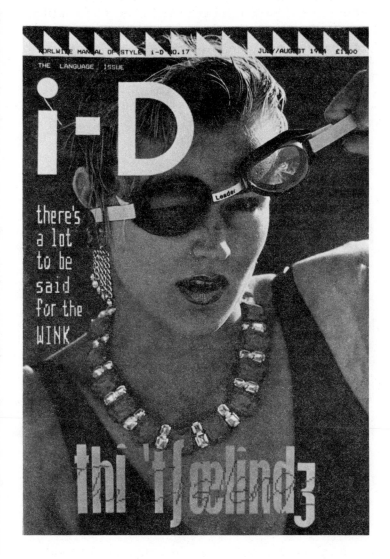

(photo: Marc Lebon for *i-D* magazine/make-up: Kay Montano)

57

(John Logan/Shadows and Light)

Riots, rights and remaking

In April 1980 there occurred a black riot in the St Paul's district of Bristol. A year later rioting broke out in the Railton Road area of Brixton, a predominantly black area of south London. In both cases, too much pressure in Britain's Shanty Towns led to a Front Line confrontation between high-profile policing and disaffected inner-city black youth.[4] The language of the Kingston ghetto, amplified by reggae music, found a home in the British black community. Those involved, usually young, unemployed black males are rarely 'immigrants' but second-generation black Britons who have discovered that they 'have merely exchanged one colonial context for another' (Pryce, 1979). The only space in which these invisible black citizens manage to be publicly represented is in the media spectacle of the street riot.

But inside these histories, inside racism, job discrimination, marginalization, urban decay, cut-backs in public spending and the policing of the subsequent crisis, there is also a major confrontation between desire and the absence of means. In a society based on consumption (whatever its moral apologists might argue) materially to deny that possibility is to invite a breakdown in its very order.

In times of economic recession, consumerism can seem a mocking image, particularly for the poor and the unemployed. The contradictions appear naked, inconfutable. The recourse to crime and rioting in various British cities by black and white youth in the summer of 1981, its resurgence in the Handsworth district of Birmingham in September 1985, and in London and Liverpool in the following weeks, seemed to converge 'on a single point of tension: desire and the absence of means, a brick and a shop window . . . The right to work subsumed in the right to consume' (Hebdige, 1982). In its cruel eloquence this situation, these actions, speak of a world where the production of one's self operates through the public signs of consumption, through a self-conscious knowledge of the logic of consumer society: an instinctive grasping of the fact that it is necessary to stamp your identity on the goods or else be stamped upon by them.

Those on the receiving end of economic change, in particular youth, are the first to experience the dislocating effects as traditional industries and their attendant services close and the small plants of the inner-city economy – whether they make shoes or micro-electronic components – migrate to Singapore, South Korea and Taiwan. In their wake they leave the bitter frustration of 'welfare economies'. The empty horizons and empty pockets of their inhabitants, sharing the same High Street as the hi-fi shops, supermarkets and clothing stores, inevitably transform such zones into sites of social warfare prone to ignite as flashpoints of violent retribution.

The diverse presence and demands of dispossessed blacks and women, the growing army of the unemployed, and the seemingly permanent installation of a lumpenproletariat, transform British urban culture into a complex and volatile pattern. Connections between popular tastes and a white, urban, male working class can no longer be assumed. Popular culture, its

(Carlo Romano/Ufficio Ricerche e Documentazione sull'Immaginario)

A black youth dressed in the rags and chains of white punks: cross-cultural dressing that confuses a simple alignment between subject and style. Assembled across his body these signs of metropolitan breakdown simultaneously expose and transform a series of different histories: urban, social, economic, racial, subcultural, generational, sexual.

tastes, sights and sounds, flows across the older lines of class. But then the idea that popular culture is simply a synonym for working–class leisure has always been an over-simplification.

Nineteenth-century popular culture was already: **inclusive, welcoming into its ambit the huge human and occupational**

variety covered by the words 'labourers, artisans, shop-keepers and tradesmen'. It cannot . . . be described as 'a working class culture', but at the same time it was imbued with a sense of popular rights. (Cunningham, 1980, 38)

Popular culture today inherits popular tastes and practices in which an urban working-class experience has often been central. But, at the same time, it stretches well beyond that classic moment of proletarian life situated somewhere between the 1880s and the eve of the Second World War. Already by the 1930s, modernism and wider urban tastes were so mixed up in the combustible language of British popular culture that America and commerce proved a far more convincing target for its critics than its native working class.[5]

And leisure, once traditionally balanced by the presence of work, acquires new meanings when work for many is being dramatically curtailed and redefined: 'having to grow up working class without work' (Cohen, 1985, 33). Major changes in the economy, the removal of traditional manual labour and industrial skill, the redeployment of production, and the effects of all this on the ecology of urban culture are immense. They induce crises both at the level of everyday life and in the previous methods employed for measuring reality; crises in political, cultural and social perspectives based on an earlier totality of sense in which 'labour' had been central.

On the margins of a shrinking, traditional working class there exist groups – girls and women in their public and private lives, unemployed black and white youth, racially discriminated communities, not to speak of an indistinct grouping of white-collar workers, intellectuals and radicals – who also claim their 'right to the city' (Henri Lefebvre).

This expansive remaking of the forces and the field of popular culture inevitably nudges and disrupts inherited categories. Contemporary popular culture may no longer be strictly 'working class' as the idealist purists of political formalism would like, but it does emerge from subordinate cultures, from the inventive edges of the consensus, from the previously ignored and suppressed. It gestures through a widening democratization of styles, signs, sounds and images, to an important remaking, to new possibilities, new perspectives, new projects.

Notes

1. Despite the controversy surrounding tower blocks, they always represented only a small percentage of public housing. And in Newcastle, for example, it was the high-rise flats that proved popular, with low-rise estates having the problem of unattended gardens overrun by packs of dogs (Esher, 1983).

2. See his trilogy of essays published in the critical arts magazine *Block*: 'Towards a cartography of taste 1935–1962', 'Object as Image: the Italian Scooter Cycle', and 'In Poor Taste'. An edited version of the first essay has also been published in Waites, Bennett and Martin (1982).

3. Janice Winship's work on women's magazines and the construction of the female 'I' in the world of consumerism is particularly important in this respect. See Winship (1981).

4. For a good analysis of the cultural economy of hustling, reggae and unemployment in the St Paul's district of Bristol, published a year before the riot, see Pryce (1979).

5. It also permitted critics sympathetic to traditional working-class culture – Orwell and Hoggart, for example – to avoid the uncomfortable fact that many of these 'foreigners' had been thoroughly naturalized; that native working-class culture and popular taste had irreversibly changed, not so much for the better or the worse, but better to meet *their* present.

Suggestions for further work

1. In the development of the contemporary British city the home and domestic architecture tended to evolve under the ideal of the 'cottage', in clear opposition to industrialism and the modernist movement in architecture. Modernism tended to find a greater welcome in urban popular culture, where it gave form to the popular imagination in cinema design, in music, dance and fashion.

What, in your opinion, lies in this distinction between

tradition and modernism; between, if you like, the commitment of urban, frequently working-class, youth to contemporary Continental fashion and the latest in American popular music and a patrician culture clinging to the traditional tastes of a romanticized national heritage: the cottage, the countryside, and nineteenth-century design?

2. Contemporary popular culture is frequently criticized for being commercial and reflecting crass tastes that are blindly driven by market forces. This situation is compared unfavourably with what is seen as a more 'authentic' urban popular culture of the late nineteenth and early twentieth centuries. Suggest why this is fundamentally an idealized view of the urban popular culture of that period.

3. Advertising occupies a central but contradictory role in urban living. It persuades you to purchase but it also offers the possibility of a purchase on change: constructing your public 'self' amongst the goods and images of the contemporary world. Try and explain this aspect with some examples.

4. The entrance of speed into daily life has been of incalculable influence, from its effects on transport, messages, images and information to the arrival of foodstuffs from faraway places. It has induced a change in all our habits: in how and where we work, in what we eat, and in what and how we consume. At the same time, this shared network continues to be crossed by signs of social distinction: the choice of supermarket, dress, magazine or newspaper; differences are maintained *within* an increasingly common framework. Still, the possibility of shared knowledge and a more democratic distribution of experiences might suggest that previously separate realities (an abstract, 'high' culture as opposed to local, working-class cultures) are in practice breaking up, with their tendencies and tastes being relocated *within* the internal differences of a more accessible and more extensive urban popular culture. What do you think?

5. The rise of present-day popular culture has, as we have seen, been marked by certain social distinctions: losing contact with a rural and urban patrician culture, it went on to be formed predominantly by those living inside the everyday realities of the nineteenth-century city – the working and lower middle classes.

Why is it that today, and certainly far less so than, say, eighty years ago, popular culture can no longer be assumed simply to represent the moment of relaxation from labour, the other side of work; or, for that matter, to be tied solely to white or male pleasures and tastes?

(Peter Osborne)

PART TWO
THE SIGHTS

4 A WORLD OF
IMAGES

... the image is not a meeting point between the real and the
imaginary but is the act that simultaneously constitutes
the real and the imaginary. (Morin, 1962)

Every day we move through a visual world of advertisements
and newspapers, photographs and magazines, cinema and
television: an optical empire that is regularly criticized for its
power to influence and shape our lives. This visual collage,
accompanying us from morning to night, is a product of the
three giant forces of the contemporary world: industrialization,
capitalism, and urbanization. And the power of the images that
these processes have produced – adverts for British beer,
Japanese hi-fi systems or Italian cars; the latest style in jacket or
skirt on *Top of the Pops* or in the pages of *She*; the drama of
televisual lives: *Dallas*, *Coronation Street*, *Brookside*, *Crossroads* – is
inescapable. They are part of daily vision, contributing to the
way we look at and understand our world. We continually select
images from the cinema, from fashion, from magazines, from
adverts, from television. They stand in for 'reality', become a
reality; the signs of experience, of self.

For many critics this simply means that we live in an
increasingly closed and 'artificial' universe, where 'false' desires
are manufactured and our tastes controlled; where the mass

69

Contemporary adverts adopt the manners of the markets and the magazines in which they appear. Pernod is clearly a drink for the 'faces', the young stylists (hip to the mythologies of 'cool': the '40s and '50s, jazz, clubbing, shades, hair gel, and Continental fashion) who peruse the pages of The Face.

media constructs the public for the product, and we 'choose', ignorant of the underlying manipulation. So, the criticism runs, the modern visual languages of advertising, photography, cinema and television have become, at best, instruments of indoctrination, at worst, instruments of surveillance (photographic records, closed circuit television, market research, data banks).

But, if 'the only world we can know is a world which is already *represented*' (Burgin, 1984), can our own desires, wants, interests, tastes and pleasures, really be assumed to be so obviously 'directed' and 'produced'?

In this section I will examine the rise of the urban 'eye', and in the next, popular music. Against a frequently negative reading of popular urban imagery and sounds I will try to suggest a different view, one based on the evidence of the translation of products, technologies and techniques into a comprehensible daily currency. For, alongside the more obvious powers of the communications industry, there also exists a story of cultural investment, innovation and transformation that has led to a popular and novel grasp of contemporary reality.

I want to suggest that what is involved in these experiences is not 'false' but the stuff of everyday sense where the pleasure, the meaning and the interest in listening to music, wearing fashions, going to the cinema, watching television, takes effect. Inside this perpetual transference between sight and sound in everyday life there are histories of choice, taste and pleasure; the story of our social, sensual and sensitized 'I's.

The mechanical eye and the dream palace

The subsequent industrialisation of camera technology only carried out a promise inherent in photography from its very beginnings: to democratise all experiences by translating them into images. (Sontag, 1979a, 7)

It is necessary to learn the objects, that is to learn to multiply on them the possible points of view. (Jean-Paul Sartre in Morin, 1956)

Photography was initially developed in the 1840s and in the following decade photographic studios specializing in portraits were in business in major urban centres. By 1861, 'there were over 200 photographic studios in London, thirty-five of them in Regent Street' (Scharf, 1975, 42). In the beginning photography was seen very much as a branch of art. Its detailed reproduction of nature often led artists to rely upon it as opposed to lengthy sittings, and by 1870 photography had almost completely replaced the work of the portrait miniaturists, although some artists found work in colouring photographs. The art academies sought to contain this new reproductive technique; meanwhile, the English art critic John Ruskin's early enthusiasm for photography turned to serious doubts. Believing that it must only serve as a handmaiden to art, Ruskin came to consider photography a serious threat which he eventually consigned to that long list making up the 'mechanical poison that this terrible nineteenth century has poured upon men' (John Ruskin in Scharf, 1975, 97).

Yet the clash between art and photography, inspiration and technology, genius and machine, was complex. Such 'eminent Victorians' as the painters Lord Leighton, Sir John Millais and Sir Lawrence Alma-Tadema were themselves deeply involved in the reproduction business. Millais, apart from selling his work to an advertising campaign (Pears' 'Bubbles' soap advert), earned up to £35,000 a year, with much of it coming from reproduction rights: 'reproduction rights that made nineteenth-century pop stars from major artists' (York, 1984, 54). As Peter York points out, these painters 'worked for reproduction, and engravings from their works went via "prints", novels and history books into every Pooter villa – and socially well below – in Victorian England. They shaped the way generations of English people saw the world' (York, 1984, 54).

But although both painting and photography could be reproduced, there remained a fundamental distinction. The engraving and the print referred back to the original painting; the reproduction was a distinct process, sanctified, as Walter Benjamin notes, by the fact that around it hung the 'aura' of the original. With the camera, however, the very mechanisms involved in taking a picture imply reproduction. A photograph does not imitate images, it reproduces them; a photograph is not 'copied', it is merely duplicated. And with the introduction of cheap photography the right to use this technology and re-present the world – its faces, objects, people, movement, happenings, all these ready-made compositions, these *images trouvées* – would become increasingly accessible. (The passage from the twenty-four-hour development of a Kodak Brownie photo to the instant Polaroid was a matter of technology, not aesthetics.)

It was in the 1880s that the hand-held Kodak camera and the cheap snapshot were introduced. The wedding photo, the seaside shot, the family group, the portrait; visual memories and keepsakes, snapshots and photographic albums, what Barthes calls 'certificates of presence', were soon part of almost every home.

Photography laid the basis of a new visual vulgate. Its tautology of objects – 'the pipe is always a pipe, inexhaustibly' (Barthes, 1981) – leads to that fascination with the image which transforms subjects into objects.

Unlike paintings, drawings and writing, photographs 'do not translate from appearances. They quote from them' (Berger and Mohr, 1982). It signals an irreversible turning point in the formation of the urban eye. If it became part of the 'technology of power' (Michel Foucault) through its employment in the compilation of criminal records, in investigative reportage, in newspapers, and in advertising, photography also began to educate the eye to consume images rather than beliefs (Barthes, 1981).[1]

While photography slowly opened up the public eye to the fascination of the image, it was the cinema, which, like the plane, took off at the beginning of this century, that dramatically plunged the viewer into a vortex of representations. It was not a train entering a station that created so much excitement amongst the first cinema audiences, but 'an image of a train' (Morin, 1965).

In an epoch of movement and modernism, with the birth of the motor car, the plane, the cinema, and total war, and with the

(Peter Osborne)

A black woman walking through the falling snow is always a black woman walking through the falling snow, inexhaustibly (after Roland Barthes).

eye captured by advertisements, speed and spectacle, the social reception of the image underwent a major extension. And it was the widespread popularity of the cinema in the first half of the twentieth century that largely helped to render this new flux of imagery navigable.

By 1914, a cinema existed on every High Street, many of them occupying previous theatres and music halls. In the late

74

1920s, when going to the 'flicks' was becoming for many people the most important social event of the week, cinemas with over 4000 seats were being constructed. Cinemas became more opulent, complete with uniformed ushers and attendants, and more fantastic. Imitating the American 'atmospheric' cinemas and their exotic Italian, Spanish and Oriental interiors, the Astorias at Finsbury Park, Brixton and Streatham that opened in the 1930s presented the public with Babylonian friezes, fountain courts and Moorish interiors. They were followed a little later by the Art Deco style of the Odeon cinemas. Many of these opulent interiors were also equipped with giant Wurlitzer organs that, rising from the depths of the orchestra pit with the organist already in full flight, entertained the audience in the intervals. Such 'picture palaces' were themselves like film sets, in dramatic contrast to their location in the working-class and suburban areas of Britain's major cities.

Fires Were Started (National Film Archive, London)

First a Girl (National Film Archive, London)

For ninepence in the 1930s you had access to four hours of entertainment, the cinema restaurant, and various social and sexual encounters. The cinema was the local entertainment centre, a place in which to enjoy yourself with soft drinks, sweets and your friends; it represented a night out, an extensive cultural experience, as well as watching a film.

Whether we like it or not, it is the movies that mould, more than any other single force, the opinions, the taste, the language, the dress, the behaviour, and even the physical appearance of a public comprising more than 60 per cent of the population of the earth. If all the serious lyrical poets, composers, painters and sculptors were forced by law to stop their activities, a rather small fraction of the general public would become aware of the fact and a still smaller fraction would seriously regret it. If the same thing were to happen with the movies the social consequences would be catastrophic. (Erwin Panofsky, in Banham, 1981, 89)

With the cinema the impact of the new visual vulgate accelerates. Time can be slowed down, speeded up, cut up, dilated and inflated, reversed and projected forwards. The cinema is a time machine. But space is also reconstructed. We pass through walls and look through roofs. Space, time and objects are metamorphosed; the cinema introduces us to a fluid universe (Jean Epstein). Its seductive realism is an 'image of the real'. All the visual tricks that later became techniques for cinematic 'realism' – the shot, the close-up, the use of lighting, and the new fluidity of time: the dissolve, the wipe, the cut, the flash-back, the montage – were developed right at the outset of the cinema. 'The equipment-free aspect of reality here has become the height of artifice; the sight of immediate reality has become an orchid in the land of technology' (Benjamin, 1973, 235).

The cinema can break every limit and rule except that of the primary objectivity of photography. This 'objectivity is the *balustrade* of the imaginary' (Morin, 1956). It presides over and establishes perception, so that the subjectivity of the senses and the objectivity of the eye become entangled. Even the music that accompanied the silent movies remained an integral part of subsequent cinema: an (unrealistic) means of illuminating the internal logic of the film's reality.

The cinema provides a space in which the reproduction of

images is opened up to personal integration. Cinema re-presents the objects and actions of the world in simultaneously symbolic and concrete form: it is a language. It offers a moment in which the seen is fused with the lived, the known with the possible, the here with the elsewhere. The cinema masticates the imaginary and digests the social. But it is the spectator who activates and feeds it. For the cinema needs more than images and all the reproductive technology and techniques that lie behind them; it requires continual participation, involvement.

. . . the tasks which face the human apparatus of perception at the turning points of history cannot be solved by optical means, that is, by contemplation, alone. They are mastered gradually by habit, under the guidance of tactile appropriation. (Benjamin, 1973, 242)

Notes

1. In the last decade of the nineteenth century the image of the body is subject to a whole series of new practices and discourses that will transform its place in the imaginary: it is photographed and then projected in the cinema, while its interior realities begin to be explored by X-rays and psychoanalysis.

5 NATIONAL VIEWS

In this chapter we will look at the formation of a particular public eye; one that offers a peculiarly 'British' slant on much of the contemporary visual media – cinema, televisions, news photos, even comics.

Ideology in the dark

Film, television and news photos are powerful media and it is tempting to analyse them in terms of power; to discover in them the logic of the economic, cultural and political interests that sustain a particular 'view' of the world, a particular ideology. In the following pages, where we look at the visual mode known as 'naturalism' and suggest its association with a certain representation of the 'British character', we will be offering such an analysis. But to argue that the cinema, for example, is *only* an ideological apparatus that serves merely to represent one particular view – 'this is how the world is', or 'this is what people are like' – is to miss the fullness of its sense and place in our everyday lives.[1]

The cinematic experience is rarely so reductive. Cinema is a social institution, a meaning machine that without an audience remains inactive. To take your seat in the dark, with its intense 'sense of closure and enclosure' that is far more radical than watching television or reading a book, is the movement that forces the film on the screen into successive meanings. There is never a 'neutral' audience (Elsaesser, 1981). It has different ages, different sexes, different social experiences. At the same time, the sense of the film is not simply left up to us to decide. In the cinema, money, meaning and pleasure collude and collide. So, the vision is structured.

We participate in cinematic temporalities, in its sequence of events, in its continuities and consequences; we are implicated in the spectacle. The optical languages and techniques used, the narrative, the style of telling, all provide us with explanatory frames. Signs and stories are organized according to the expectancies of narrative and genre: violence acquires different meanings in a Western, a musical and a horror film. As Steven Neale points out, recognizing the genre offers a semantic passage through a film that could otherwise suffer from incoherence under an excess of possible meanings (Neale, 1981). Of course, you can be involved in a film in various ways, not all of them welcome or pleasurable. More simply, a film can be considered 'nonsense' or 'rubbish', and left at that.

What I am trying to suggest is that what we experience in the cinema can rarely be reduced to an ideological message, bare and simple. In the dark, gaps are opened that are not always satisfactorily 'resolved' with the ending of the film: they stick in the memory; they attract, repel, shock, and surprise us. It is this which suggests that the sense of the film invariably slips beyond ideological arrest. It therefore also suggests the possibility of re-reading British cinema – both its realist and fantasy sides – in a more open-ended manner (Higson, 1983).

So, looking at British cinema involves a two-fold task: rescuing what has been critically marginalized (those 'other views'), which we will try to do in the next chapter when we examine Gainsborough melodrama, Hammer horror and the burlesque comedy of the 'Carry On' films, and re-viewing it all in terms of popular pleasure and appropriation.

Films do not only provide ideological solutions. They may well do this, but they also do more; and it is that 'more' which makes a film more than merely ideological, that makes it a rich cultural event rather than simply a 35mm version of an existing socio-political consensus.

The rise of Hollywood

Celluloid film was an American invention, and while in the early 1900s experiments with film were going on in Europe, particularly in France with the Lumière brothers and Georges Méliès, one of the first films with a plot and a narrative arrived from across the Atlantic in 1903. It was E. S. Porter's *The Great Train Robbery*.

The Great Train Robbery (National Film Archive, London)

In Britain there was initially a lot of resistance to taking the cinema seriously, and, no doubt to counteract its fairground-style novelty and lowly associations, when material was chosen

81

it was inevitably from the sanctified realms of literature (Shakespeare, Dickens, Hardy) or history (the Civil War, Queen Victoria).

But the success of D. W. Griffith's *The Birth of a Nation* (1915) had irreversible effects on the cinema throughout the world. The British public rapidly came to prefer the better made and more varied US films to inferior native efforts. In 1920, out of a total of 878 films available only 144 were British, and six years later only 5 per cent of screen time was occupied by British material (Perry, 1975, 47). This finally led to protectionist measures and the establishment of a quota system. Under this arrangement British cinemas were obliged to turn over a part of their screen time to showing British-made films: 5 per cent in 1927 when the quota was established, rising to 20 per cent in 1936.[2] Hollywood had meanwhile developed the highly cinematic genres of the Western, the comic, and the epic, and put together an independent universe illuminated by its own 'star system', its

Intolerance (National Film Archive, London)

'vamps', lovers and 'sweethearts', its comics, cowboys and, later, cartoons.[3]

The attempts made by the British film industry to resist the popular language of Hollywood was a muddled affair, deeply compromised by its own uncertainty about the status and nature of cinema. Labouring under the weight of a native literary tradition and theatrical establishment, the young medium frequently had difficulty in establishing its own voice and vision. Caught up in older traditions of representation, it often remained distant from the more fragmentary and visually faster approach involved in the mechanical constructed drama of cinema that was being largely pioneered in California, and which invariably peaked in the historical sweep and grandeur of the epic or the outdoor chase sequence of the Western, comic or gangster film.

The coming of sound seemed to offer new hope to the Quota Companies. Surely even Americans would prefer the nicely enunciated English of RADA-trained actors to the coarse utterances of the hitherto popular screen players? British exhibitors knew their audiences rather better and became increasingly vociferous over the unpopular British films they were obliged to show to fulfil quota provisions. In the north of England and Scotland, the lah-di-dah accents of British actors aroused derision and hostility while the racy vivacity of American slang quickly became a vital part of popular culture . . . one East End exhibitor reported that his patrons 'like good pictures, good American pictures, pictures of movement and action. They won't stand British pictures here at any price'. (Murphy, 1983, 98)

Representing Britain

Belated attempts to change this situation and to compete directly with Hollywood were launched in the 1930s by Alexander Korda, and a decade later by J. Arthur Rank. In both cases, the failure to overcome the massive problems of breaking into the lucrative American market – necessary to justify the high production costs of the spectacular films they envisaged – eventually curtailed their ambitions. In the end, a British cinema of this type, however more tasteful and realistic it claimed to be, could rarely offer any competition to the financial and artistic masters of that style, Hollywood.

However, in 1933 at Radio City Music Hall in New York, Alexander Korda premiered *The Private Life of Henry VIII*. It was a major success and launched Korda on a series of costume dramas: *Catherine the Great*, *The Private Life of Don Juan*, *The Scarlet Pimpernel*, *Rembrandt*. He supplemented these films with imperialist spectacles – *Sanders of the River*, *The Four Feathers* – where white heroes with names like Sanders, Carruthers and Feversham (the quiet, public-school authority of such names almost rings with moral superiority), aided by their trusty

The Private Life of Henry VIII (National Film Archive, London)

servants, were constantly putting down rebellion in the far reaches of the Empire.[4] The *New York Times* christened the Hungarian Korda 'the Kipling of the kinema'.

In the 1930s, there was also the successful partnership of producer Michael Balcon with directors Alfred Hitchcock – *The Man Who Knew Too Much*, *The Thirty-Nine Steps*, *The Secret Agent*, *Sabotage* – and Victor Saville with the Jessie Matthews musicals: *Evergreen*, *First a Girl*, *It's Love Again*. But these films form part of a more modest local success, alongside the comedy and song of George Formby, Gracie Fields and Will Hay. The Hitchcock thriller achieved fame via Hollywood and not Balcon's company, Gaumont-British.

The British films of the 1930s had now to compete with the established international style of sumptuous American musicals, the glittering symmetry of Busby Berkeley's cinematic follies, the gangster, the Western, and the Hollywood 'superstars' of the period: Fred Astaire and Ginger Rogers, Clark Gable, Gary Cooper, Joan Crawford, Claudette Colbert, Carole Lombard, Jean Arthur, Cary Grant.

It was above all this mythological 'America' that transformed the cinema into a dream palace, a self-referring world that offered refuge and imaginative alternatives to urban and suburban life in Britain in the 1930s.

The exaltation of the 'British character', both in Korda's epics and in the down-to-earth, Northern working-class humour and common sense revealed in the films of Gracie Fields and George Formby, was undoubtedly popular. But it was also against the limits and direct experiences of those traditions that Hollywood proved so fresh, novel, stimulating, sophisticated and, ultimately, so culturally subversive. Which is not to dismiss those native traditions, only to suggest that Hollywood and certain baroque forms of later British cinema – Gainsborough costumed melodramas and Hammer horror, for example – may be as important to our understanding of 'British cinema' as representations of working-class life and imperialist destiny. And let us be even more explicit: Brando's mumble, John Ford's deserts, Cary Grant's uncrumpled Brooks Brothers suit and Joan Crawford's arched eyebrows are also part of *our* cinema.

The Thirty-Nine Steps (National Film Archive, London)

. . . consider the hero of two comparable Alfred Hitchcock films, both chase-movies. In the pre-war *39 Steps* the hero wore tweeds and got a little rumpled as the chase wore on, like a gentleman farmer after a day's shooting. In *North by North West* (1959) the hero is an advertising man (a significant choice of profession) and though he is hunted from New York to South Dakota his clothes stay neatly Brooks Brothers. That is to say, the dirt, sweat and damage of pursuit are less important than the package in which the hero comes – the tweedy British gentleman or the urbane Madison Avenue man. (Alloway, 1959, 41–2)

(Carlo Romano/Ufficio Ricerche e Documentazione sull'Immaginario)

However, between local humour, imperialist fairy tales and historical pageantry, there existed a further native perspective. This was the documentary film movement. Influenced by early Soviet cinema and later by the research into everyday Britain carried out by Mass Observation, the documentary film movement is usually associated with the names of John Grierson and Humphrey Jennings.[5] Taking cinema to be a potentially 'democratic institution' (John Grierson), the movement attempted to widen the cultural lens of the 1930s and wartime Britain through its documentary realist style.

Central to the documentary movement was the belief that film recorded 'the real world'. Such naive realism was no doubt refreshing alongside the artifice of musicals, historical dramas and romance that both mainstream British cinema and Hollywood preferred to present. But whether it is the camera 'capturing' the performance of Charles Laughton in *Rembrandt*, or the faces and actions of the nameless actors in Grierson's *Drifters* and Jennings's *Listen to Britain*, the mode of representation remains strikingly similar. Although an initial definition would be realism, this 'realism is best understood in terms of what it was *not*, what it set itself against – namely notions of fantasy, melodrama, glamour and Hollywood' (Medhurst, 1985, 4). Such a 'realism' has pretensions beyond a merely visual style: it is anti-Hollywood and anti-glamour. It rests on a set of social and cultural definitions in which the camera is considered a neutral means for 'recording' the 'real world' of social events or

Drifters (National Film Archive, London)

. . . it has to be said that the images of workers in such films had an extraordinary effect. It is difficult to convey to people to whom shots of workers are the routine images of television documentaries, the impact of such pictures on audiences in the thirties; as Grierson records, their appearance on the screen caused spontaneous applause from spectators used to the representation of workers in British feature films, in which, as Ralph Bond, a Communist member of the movement has explained, 'when workers did appear . . . they were always the comedy relief, the buffoons, the idiots or the servants'. (Hood, 1983, 108)

observing the acting. Optics, and the pragmatic limits of a liberal, empiricist culture – the world is smply 'there', to be observed, filmed and reproduced – are combined in a diffused 'naturalism'. The result is quite distinctly not 'Hollywood'; it is a 'British way of seeing'.

Listen to Britain (National Film Archive, London)

The power and strength of naturalism in the visual media is undeniable. In the same period, for example, the British magazine *Picture Post* developed a photo-reporting style that, drawing upon the documentary film movement, Mass Observation, the newly founded Left Book Club, and radical popular journalism, successfully caught the restless world of the 1930s and the participatory populism of the war. The 'eye' of *Picture Post* formed part of the literary (and real) road to the 'people', to Wigan Pier, to the pub, to the dangers of fascism and Munich, to the experiences of the Blitz.[6] But, as Stuart Hall has pointed out, the magazine's 'naturalism', while resplendent in the ordinary accents of everyday experience, lacked 'a language of dissent, opposition or revolt' (Hall, 1972). This was finally its strength and weakness.

As a *mode* of representation, naturalism invariably confuses its own construction with reality itself. It leads to a closed universe, ultimately incapable of acknowledging other views and real differences in the world it seeks slavishly to reproduce. Because it 'records reality' it can only absorb, not challenge, existing social visions.

(Carlo Romano/Ufficio Ricerche e Documentazione sull'Immaginario)

Further evidence of the constructed ethos involved in a 'national vision' comes from another source: that of the successful campaign waged in the early 1950s against American horror, crime and war comics. The campaign waged by the Comics Campaign Council (actually a British Communist Party front), and then taken up by the National Union of Teachers, was, as Martin Barker points out, 'about a conception of society, children and Britain' (Barker, 1984).[7] It led to the 1955 Children and Young Persons (Harmful Publications) Act which still remains law today. The campaign was directed against an American vision, against a 'world' in which 'nothing is sacred, everything was corrupt' (Barker, 1984); against the threat to British culture of a debased, commercial culture that offered with Classic Comics, for instance, a Macbeth *told 'in the modern manner . . . streamlined for action'. According to* Picture Post, *in 1954 more than 300 million comics were sold in Britain each year; not all of them were of the likes of* Eagle, Girl, Beano *and* Topper. *The clean-cut Dan Dare and tubby Digby locked in open struggle with the evil machinations of the Mekon was quite different from '. . . a terrible twilight zone between sanity and madness, an area peopled by monsters, grave robbers, human flesh eaters', provided in such US publications as* Tales from the Crypt *and* Eerie. *With their twists, surprise endings and shock effects, the American comics disrupted a lot of the assumed innocence of childhood and social stereotyping projected by the British publications and their moral guardians.[8]*

More frequently, the naturalist assumptions of the camera's eye are rarely so tested by daily events, preferring, at least in cinema and television, to dwell on shots of a stylized Englishness: a 'conservative dream world . . . far more synthetic than the most plastic products of Hollywood' (Nairn, 1981, 261). The move from the native cinema of the 1930s to the contemporary narrative form, television, has involved no sharp transition in visual style. The chaotic menace of the present is eschewed for the tasteful immobility of naturalism and the quiet authority of the past, preserved in the 'great tradition' of native history and literature. The list of televised historical drama is interminable: *The Forsyte Saga, Elizabeth R, Upstairs, Downstairs, Churchill's People, Poldark, Brideshead Revisited*; since 1950 the BBC has prepared more than thirty separate adaptations of Dickens. Variations on this exportable heritage have recently become the basis for the re-launching of a spectacular British cinema that once again maintains a 'tasteful' distance from the excesses of Hollywood: *Chariots of Fire*, *Gandhi*, *A Passage to India*.

The photography is beautiful (in the very best colour supplement way), ravishingly lovely, with the kind of luminousness that you only get with perfect colour prints on a big screen. The timing of each shot is impeccable, lingering long enough to register the beauty of a landscape but not so long as to hold up the unfolding of the story. The acting is nuanced, detailed, carefully observed, exquisitely rounded. Everything in the film is in place – which also means that everything in the film is neatly parcelled up. (Dyer, 1985, 44)

Pleasurable viewing, but inside the optical 'realism', inside this technicolour evocation of an 'English vision', we find ourselves descending into a subconscious pattern of cultural smugness: a crippling spectacle whose narrow limits are lost in that parochial romanticism which is the principal vehicle for the 'cryptic nature of English nationalism' (Nairn, 1981, 79). And while literary sources lend the aura of 'art' to the proceedings, contemporary events – the Royal Wedding, the Falklands war – are translated into contemporary extensions of the televised national epic.

This 'eye', convinced that it is a universal measure, produces a perspective whose aesthetic and cultural concerns set the terms of normal vision. Real differences, be they racial, sexual, and otherwise social, are reduced to a tolerant landscape 'based on a complacent assumption that we're all the same anyway' (Dyer, 1985).

Of course, there is another side to these 'national visions' and their ideology: the side that some might label 'kitsch' (see next chapter), but, above all, the side that could be popularly associated with soap opera. (The perpetual interest of the public and the press in the public doings and private transgressions of the Royal Family is of course the real life soap of the 'Windsor Dynasty'.) For the costumed sign – from Korda's *Henry VIII* to *The Jewel in the Crown* – has two faces; on one side there is the static reassurance of 'naturalism', on the other there is melodrama, romance and soap. Which sounds suspiciously like Hollywood, American television and British 'bad taste'.

Notes

1. For a further discussion on ideology and the limits of ideological analysis, see chapter 11.

2. This system gave a major boost to the British film industry. But it did not necessarily mean that these films, often hastily made and shoddily finished ('quota quickies'), were as popular or as competent as their US rivals. However, by 1937 British film production had become the second highest in the world after that of the United States.

3. The 'star system' was invented in Hollywood between 1910 and 1920. Small film studios fighting the grip of the major studios on the fledgling industry discovered the public interest in certain faces and actors. They rapidly transmuted this interest into stable collateral for future film production: exclusive contracts were signed, images promoted, publicity invented, and the star system was launched (Dyer, 1979a).

4. *Sanders of the River* was justly satirized three years later, in 1938, in comedian Will Hay's *Old Bones of the River*.

5. As Robert Colls and Philip Dodd have noted, the Documentary Movement, and Grierson's views in particular, can be directly linked to the 'Into Unknown England' social reportage of the late nineteenth century (Colls and Dodd, 1985). Add to this the 'Free Cinema' and the 'working-class realist' cinema of the late 1950s and early 1960s and we have a remarkable continuity in themes, ideological vision and cultural consensus that could, without being too unfair, be dubbed the social conscience of British 'naturalism'.

6. The obvious documents here are Orwell's *Road to Wigan Pier*, the Mass Observation book, *The Pub and the People*, and Humphrey Jennings's film, *Fires Were Started*.

7. Barker relates the story of Alan Poole, a 'youthful gangster from Chatham' who died in a gun battle with the police in his 'hideout full of gunman comic books' (Barker, 1984, 30), as part of the public evidence being presented on the evil influences arriving from across the ocean. In fact, one Western comic had been found, and 'not a very alarming one'.

8. See Barker 1984, 159–69, for details.

6 OTHER VISIONS, SCREENS AND PLEASURES

In the post-war world, once again faced with a flood of American films, many of which were held up by the hostilities, British critics struggled to find an alternative in 'quality' British films. Against the glamorous power of the Hollywood star system and the individual popularities of Tyrone Power, Victor Mature, Judy Garland, Jane Russell and Ava Gardner, the critics' choice usually fell on films that dealt 'realistically' with the war (*Western Approaches, In Which We Serve, The Way To The Stars*), the classics (*Henry V, Great Expectations*), or an 'adult film expressing an essential Englishness' such as the self-denying fortitude of the two lovers in David Lean's *Brief Encounter* (Perry, 1975).

Convinced that 'good' cinema should follow the tone, feeling and rules of 'good' literature, and reach for 'the maturity of the Shakespearian theatre or of the best nineteenth-century novels' (Hunt, 1964), citics tended to praise a highly selective native taste, formed in another, very different, medium. The use of literary values in discussing cinema while revealing a certain paucity in the critical languages then available also provided the necessary cultural authority – 'Shakespeare's theatre',

Waterloo Road (National Film Archive, London)

Waterloo Road *(1944): the sort of native realism that was less welcomed by the critics, that of London low life and 'spivs'.*

'nineteenth-century novels' – to combat the 'false' world of celluloid stars and Hollywood. It allowed the critical discussion of cinema to continue largely unchanged in newspapers and magazines, without having really to engage with the object of its criticism. This failure to respond to the language of cinema has meant that British film culture has usually lacked both the Continental investment in the medium as an intellectual and critical art and the more nonchalent craftsmanship of Hollwood.

'Free cinema' and the subsequent working-class 'realist' films of the late 1950s and early 1960s, considered by many the high point of post-war British cinema, were, for example, characteristically both anti-theoretical and anti-Hollywood. In a fashion very similar to the documentary film movement of the 1930s and the eye of *Picture Post*, the principal concern of directors Lindsay Anderson and Karel Reisz was a commitment to a portrayal of contemporary society. In the films, drawn from successful novels or plays, *Room at the Top*, *Saturday Night and Sunday Morning*, *This Sporting Life*, *A Taste of Honey*, all the assumptions of a native naturalism were once again present in the idea of simply showing 'reality' and letting it speak 'for itself'.

Saturday Night and Sunday Morning (National Film Archive)

In the British cinema of the '50s the explicit sexuality of the posed male

97

body was frequently circumvented by a native 'manliness' that Andy
Medhurst characterizes as the 'hegemony of the tweed jacket',
personified in actors like Kenneth More, Jack Hawkins and Richard
Todd (Medhurst, 1985). James Mason had been an exception, but then
he went to Hollywood. It was eventually challenged by the Northern
town pictures of the late 1950s and early '60s, and the explicit virility of
their rebellious working-class heroes (Albert Finney, Richard Harris).

But letting things speak for themselves also meant reproducing the
dominant accents of male sexuality. The films, shot in documentary-
realist black and white and intent on showing 'how it is', tended to
reveal an 'aggressively heterosexual tradition' (Medhurst, 1985) and an
underlying structure of misogyny, where wider social textures were
frequently reduced to 'iconography and "atmosphere"' (Hill, 1983).

Against the limits of this native realism, Hollywood, American
comics, certain native film genres, and later television 'light
entertainment', have offered more exotic, sometimes bolder,
and invariably more seductive, visions.[1]

The popular iconography of an imaginary 'America' was
continually encountered in the cinema, in the B-feature world of
detective and science fiction stories; in Disney, Popeye, and
Tom and Jerry cartoons; in costumed melodramas; in *Marvel*
and *Classics Illustrated* comics; in television serials; in the sounds
and imagery of rock'n'roll and pop music. This was the 'Pop
Kultch' against which defenders of 'Britishness' railed. It was
also the source for alternative, popular forms and tastes. And for
the many who attended the cinema in the 1940s, and in declining
numbers in the 1950s and 1960s, the real alternative to the
narrow, moral tones of British naturalism and its culture came
from a suburb of Los Angeles.

Hollywood cinema is frequently criticized for giving the film-
goer a closed representation of the world; its narrative logic
apparently removes the ground for alternative interpretations.
This is sometimes referred to as the 'classic realist text': all the
filmic elements point towards a single way of understanding the
events portrayed (MacCabe, 1981).[2] The film dutifully reflects
the narrative structure and reproduces the authority of coherence.
Yet, at the same time, we instinctively understand – and this

gives rise to our pleasure – that the musical, the Western, the comedy, the thriller, the adventure, horror and science-fiction film, all push against the constraints of what we in our everyday experience understand to be 'realistic'. Hollywood rarely pretends to mirror the world, but pushes the ordinary into the extraordinary.

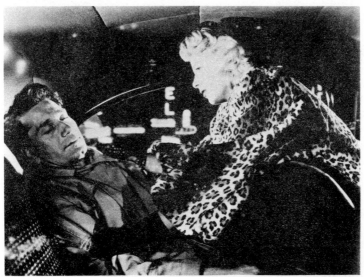

Cry of the City (National Film Archive, London)

The real city, one might say, produces only criminals; the imaginary city produces the gangster: he is what we want to be and what we are afraid we may become. (Warshow (1962)

In the following pages there are brief descriptions of certain types of film that, despite the frequent disapproval of the critics, proved popular in British cinemas between the mid-1940s and the early 1960s. Not all of them came from Hollywood. Alongside the popularity of Hollywood and the Saturday morning matinée of American cartoons, comedies and serial thrillers for children, there was also an alternative popular 'Englishness' found in the Gainsborough costumed melodramas

99

of the 1940s, Hammer horror, and various comedy cycles, in particular the 'Carry On' series.

'deadly but sexy, exciting and strong'

In the second half of the 1940s there appeared a series of American thriller films, shot in black and white and an 'uniquely sensual visual style' (Place, 1980), known as 'film noir'.[3] The 'darkness' of these films was linked to their disturbing female protagonists. The women represented a dangerous desirability that could reduce men to a state of impotence. Barbara Stanwyck in *Double Indemnity*, and Jane Greer in *Out of the Past*, Rita Hayworth in *Lady from Shanghai*, are 'dark ladies' who are ultimately unknowable, or else known at a supreme cost: desire runs into the death and destruction of the male. As the dying

Double Indemnity (National Film Archive, London)

What does the dark night hold? – a treacherous blonde and the death of the male.

Walter Neff concludes at the end of *Double Indemnity*: 'I didn't get the woman and I didn't get the money'.

The equation of female sexuality and power with evil was not only a cinematic sign, it clearly drew on wider currents. The world of film noir is a world in which women are frequently beyond the home and family, the woman being absorbed not simply in a job or career, but, that ultimate transgression, her 'self'. Viewed from this angle, these films indirectly express male fears of the disturbing female mobility that had been released by the domestic upheaval of war, economic change, new patterns of consumption and the subsequent questioning of pre-existing roles.

The filched kiss

I simply revel in bold, bad men. (Female typist referring to James Mason in *The Man in Grey*)

At that time they were the only entertainment people had, and they were entertaining, they were I suppose the equivalent of *Coronation Street*. (Betty Box, Gainsborough producer)

A contemporary British development that also involved themes of sexual stereotyping and (in)security was the series of very popular films produced by Gainsborough Studios. These films were costumed melodramas, many adapted from female romances: *The Man in Grey, They Were Sisters, Madonna Of the Seven Moons, The Wicked Lady, Caravan*. The romance provided the brooding male sexuality of James Mason, along with the swashbuckling Stewart Granger and the sardonic Dennis Price. But, if the threatened male was largely absent, the active female protagonist was not. Where film noir was strikingly contemporary in its themes and manners, the Gainsborough films usually relied on the exotic licence of distant times and foreign parts – seventeenth-century England, Victorian London, Italy, Spain – to permit the expression of female independence.

The Wicked Lady (National Film Archive, London)

Once again, these films appeared in the context of the dislocating experiences of war, where 'women and men were often thrown, literally, into each other's arms: they were squashed into shelters, tackled anti-aircraft guns together, dug out friends from debris, clutched each other in the blackout, or simply enjoyed a dance together, possibly after years of self-denial' (Minns, 1980, 178). The overall effect of war, with women working the land and the assembly lines as well as being in the armed forces, and with a general increase in sexual promiscuity, was destined to produce uncertainties in the images of post-war womanhood. As Sue Harper notes, the 'glamour' of the seventeenth-century dresses and the invitation to 'unspeakable' passions are part of a response to the war-time restrictions of utility clothing – Margaret Lockwood's costume in *The Wicked Lady* parallels the Paris fashion shows of 1946 and Dior's 'New Look' of 1947 which also 'emphasized the waist, breasts and a swirling largesse of skirt' – and 'a representation, through "costume narrative", of a female sexuality denied expression through conventional social forms' (Harper, 1983, 50).

That these films, often contemptuously referred to as 'women's films', permitted forms of expression and sentiment not allowed in the then contemporary 'realist' cinema is inadvertently exposed in the critical language of the generally hostile reviews:

Caravan (National Film Archive, London)

This is a highly osculatory piece, comprising the kiss filched, the kiss rejected, the kiss maternal, the kiss paternal, the kiss devout, the kiss marital, the kiss passionate, the kiss jealous, the kiss moribund, the gypsy kiss and the kiss of the bright young thing. These exercises are worked into a story about a Roman matron who finds periodical relaxation by throwing herself into the life of a Florentine fly-by-night. Schizophrenia, however, is not enough; and we have also a lounge lizard hand-in-glove with a gang of cutpurses, a jewel fence, a thieves' kitchen, an Embassy and a spot of Carnival. (*The Sunday Times*, 17 December 1944)

We can read the signs, the images of women in these years, in cinema, advertising, magazines, and later television, in different ways. They can be condemned for their reduction of women to abstract objects of sex, to the powerless victims of the male gaze. But, without removing that condemnation, there is more. Cutting across, through and cutting up the public iconography of their sex, and drawing upon the resulting fragments, a 'woman's discourse' has suggested further dimensions that lie beyond the mirrors of the male world. The ambiguities and pleasures of Gainsborough melodrama or women's magazines or fashion can slip beyond the male grasp to be rediscovered in the formations of femininity, feminism and the daily passage of the female 'I' through the images and goods where she is continually being re-presented.

A fate worse than death

In the cinema, the Gothic element, with its mixture of the thriller and costumed melodrama, has been consistently present: from the German expressionist cinema of the 1920s (*The Cabinet of Dr Caligari*, *The Golem*, *Nosferatu*) and Hollywood horror in the '30s, with Bela Lugosi, Boris Karloff and Lon Chaney (*Frankenstein*, *Dracula*, *White Zombie*), to the US horror/science-fiction films of the '50s, Britain's Hammer horror and the reprise of a flamboyant Gothic style in Roger Corman's Poe cycle of films in the early 1960s: *The House of Usher*, *The Pit and the Pendulum*, *The Masque of the Red Death*, and others.

In Britain, it was the popularity of the *Quatermass Xperiment* (1954), itself based on the highly successful BBC television series, *The Quatermass Experiment*, that revealed to Hammer the rich vein of horror films. Working in the B-feature market and making films of well-known subjects, drawn from radio shows (*PC 49*, *Dick Barton*) and popular mythology (Robin Hood, Dick Turpin and, of course, Baron Frankenstein and Count Dracula), were the secrets of Hammer's initial success.

It was Hammer's *Curse of Frankenstein* (1956), directed by Terence Fisher, and starring Peter Cushing, Hazel Court and Christopher Lee 'as the creature', that launched British horror film on an international commercial success without precedent in the British cinema. This cinematic 'Transylvania' constantly slid between the excesses of 'kitsch' and the self-conscious irony of 'camp'. When Christopher Lee later portrayed Dracula, his suave blend of horror and sexuality suggested a poetics of decadence, 'a hypnotic anthology of perversions', where a 'fate worse than death' had 'all the makings of an acceptable alternative to conventional life and sexuality' (Punter, 1980, 362).

The Curse of Frankenstein (National Film Archive, London)

The horror genre, although drawing upon the respect due to literary precedents (Mary Shelley, Bram Stoker, Edgar Allan Poe), has invariably been considered the territory of 'kitsch' and 'camp'. Hammer's parade of horrors, and Roger Corman's baroque landscapes inhabited by crazedly perched castles on surf-lashed cliffs and the tomb-like timbres of Vincent Price's voice, have regularly encouraged the use of such adjectives. But the two terms come out of an altogether wider debate. They emerged in the response of an elite, European culture to the widespread reproducibility of art, to the arrival of the mass media, and

(Carlo Romano/Ufficio Ricerche e Documentazione sull'Immaginario)

to the subsequent invasion of culture by popular tastes and sentiments.

Kitsch is a manner of referring to the problem of 'taste' in the contemporary world. It can be considered as a sort of optimistic gloss that locates pleasurable sensations in everything, from works of art to the pattern of a tablecloth. Everything is reduced to an accessible aesthetics: the 'classics' translated into cinema and comics, symphonic music into films scores, novels into the Reader's Digest. *Camp is more complex. It is more removed, more ironic, more refined, than kitsch. Unlike kitsch, it is not sentimental but detached. It involves the self-knowledge of artifice and stylization; it is the 'lie that tells the truth' (Jean Cocteau). If kitsch is 'bad taste', then camp, as Susan Sontag puts it, is 'the good taste of bad taste'. (Dallas is kitsch, Dynasty is camp.)*

Both kitsch and camp were terms coined for dealing with the world of urban popular culture, mass art and the democratization of taste. Both were elaborated in the world of 'high' art and its culture. But while kitsch functions fundamentally as the external, negative judgement of the critic on the margins of popular culture, camp directly engages with popular tastes by trying to aesthetize them. 'Camp is the answer to the problem: how to be a dandy in the age of mass culture' (Sontag, 1979b, 116). So, camp still maintains a distance between its own selective appropriation and the wider, everyday movement of popular culture. Its self-legitimation and secret codes – to ask for a definition of 'camp' is to be automatically excluded from its sensibility – has provided an autonomous aesthetics that has proved particularly attractive to gay culture.[4]

The incongruous presence of the horror genre in the assumed rationalities of the world forced the naturalist eye of the British cinema to break bounds. The disturbing mixture of science and occultism, of reason and terror, of rational civilization and nature's freaks, set loose a series of cycles: alongside Frankenstein (Peter Cushing) and Dracula (Christopher Lee), there was the 'Mummy' cycle (Boris Karloff), the 'Werewolf' cycle (Lon Chaney Jnr), and the 'Jekyll and Hyde' cycle.

Future dread: it came from . . .

In the same B-film world of the '50s, more contemporary terrors – an 'imagination of disaster' (Susan Sontag) – were consistently present in sci-fi films, most of them American. Many of these seemed to be fuelled by fears of shrinking security in an atomic-Cold War age. The plots were paranoiacally organized around the presence of an 'alien', a 'beast', who disrupts the conventional patterns of the 'community'.

The most famous of these films was Don Siegel's *Invasion of the Body Snatchers*. The genre enjoyed further success through the popularity on British TV of the American series *The Outer Limits*.

Although it is easy to trace the thematics of the Cold War in these films, a more complex theme was an implicit criticism of science and its apparently uncontrollable powers in a nuclear age. Meddling scientists disturbed nature – the 'beast' itself – and, releasing powers beyond their control, placed the human

107

(Carlo Romano/Ufficio Ricerche e Documentazione sull'Immaginario)

The beast may come from the stars or from 20,000 fathoms, from Mars or from beneath the earth, from the moon, Venus, the ocean floor or the black lagoon (*Flying Disc Men from Mars* (1950), *Radar Men from the Moon* (1952), *War of the Worlds* (1952), *The Beast from 20,000 Fathoms* (1953), *It Came from Outer Space* (1953), *Invaders from Mars* (1953), *Killers from Space* (1953), *Creature from the Black Lagoon* (1954), *The Monster from the Ocean Floor* (1954), to name but a few), but wherever it comes from it generally might as well have not bothered: the moral virtues of the clean-cut American hero, sometimes backed up by clean-cut American tanks and guided missiles, prove too strong – or unattractive – for it to withstand. (Punter, 1980, 352)

race in jeopardy. In the terminology of the '50s, 'boffins' or 'brains' were valuable but dangerous beings. One never knew where their investigations might take them (or us). The scientist no longer creates a Frankenstein, but becomes one, for example,

108

when atom-bomb testing shifts the Earth's axis, sending the planet spinning into the sun towards an apocalyptic fry-up in the British film, *The Day The Earth Caught Fire* (1961).

Home humours

So, where the predictable eye of British naturalism tended to be abandoned was in melodrama, horror and, finally, comedy, British comedy films went through a cycle of styles, from the 'gormless' Northern provincialism of George Formby and the blustering school-master figure of Will Hay in the 1930s, through the Ealing comedies' post-war presentation of the 'British character' and 'sense of humour' (*Passport to Pimlico, The Man in the White Suit, Kind Hearts and Coronets, The Ladykillers*), to the belly laugh vulgarity of the 'Carry On' series and the Chaplinesque antics of Norman Wisdom and Charlie Drake in the late 1950s and early '60s. In a more restrained vein, but equally drawing humour from certain British quirks, were such

Carry on Camping (National Film Archive, London)

109

successes as *Genevieve* and the *Doctor in the House* series, starring Dick Bogarde.

But the more decisive, because they were an embarrassment to 'serious' cinema, were the 'Carry On' films. The first was *Carry On Sergeant* (1958). It launched a series that became a movie continuation of the Donald McGill saucy seaside postcards of the 1930s, 'a sort of sub-world of smacked bottoms' which, like the music hall and the stand-up comedian, was 'a sort of saturnalia, a harmless rebellion against virtue' (Orwell, 1970, vol. 2).

The films were naughty postcards translated into filmic narrative and a stream of sexually motivated puns. The busty blonde, the leering wide-boy, the frustrated matron, the hen-pecked husband, the camp homosexual, were a set of (frequently offensive) pub humour stereotypes in a context that was ultimately concerned not with promiscuity or licentious behaviour, but with marriage and moral stability. The humour arose from acknowledging and joking with the repressed.

The everyday screen

Everyone is a television critic. (Hobson, 1982)

While the 1950s still presented a native cinema of laughs and screams, together with Hollywood stars and American B-features (sci-fi, horror, crime, beach and music movies – many aimed at a new 'teenage' audience), the subsequent decade witnessed a thorough shift in the cinema under the impact of television.

In the 1930s and '40s, dancing and going to the cinema were probably the two most popular events of the week. In 1946, cinema attendance in Britain peaked with 635 million admissions to 4700 cinemas. Twenty-five years later it was 163 million admissions to 1480 cinemas.

By the 1960s, bingo was being introduced as a cheap and popular substitute to fill the increasingly empty auditoria.

Alternatively, the buildings were converted, sometimes into two or three smaller cinemas, or else abandoned the merchandizing of dreams altogether and offered more direct services as supermarkets, warehouses, or car parks.

When a cinema was converted it often became an 'entertainment centre', incorporating a cinema, bar and dance floor. And it is the concept of 'entertainment' that most significantly marks the change in social habits involved in the demise of the cinema. This change arises with the popular establishment of television in the late 1950s as the privileged screen. Its dailiness, as opposed to the exceptional, the occasion, the 'night out', introduced a completely new dynamic into visual entertainment and pleasure. The uninterrupted 'flow' (Williams, 1974) of television programmes, later accentuated by a choice of channels, with flicking between them permitted by the remote-control command, augments 'discontinuous ways of seeing' (Susan Sontag). It puts earlier ideas of entertainment, tied to the coherence of a plot, a sequential narrative, and undivided attention, under increasing pressure.

Faced with the distracted eye, cinema since the 1950s has responded with the spectacular effect. There was first the adoption of colour and various wide-screen formats in the 1950s. Then there was an increasing reliance on the blockbuster (leading to the revival of the war film: *The Longest Day, A Bridge Too Far, Apocalypse Now*), the disaster genre (*Towering Inferno, Earthquake*, the 'Airport' cycle), the stomach-churning special effects of the horror film (*The Exorcist, Altered States, Friday the 13th*), science-fiction and futurology (the glittering hardware and aseptic vision of *2001*, the ironic summation of the genre in the various *Star Wars*, the baroque, post-modernist ruins of *Alien, Escape From New York, Blade Runner, Dune*, and the post-apocalyptic deserts of the *Mad Max* series). The costs involved have resulted in an increasingly 'international' cinema style.

One of the earliest examples of this widespread 'spectacularity' was the James Bond cycle. The first film, *Dr No* (1962), which starred Sean Connery and Ursula Andress, has been succeeded by a series of films in which the gadgetry becomes more ingenious, the special effects more researched, the characters increasingly iconic, with the thin line of the narrative providing a connective excuse between the images.

Even Harry Palmer, the cynical, working-class London spy of *The Ipcress File*, the slightly down-at-heel antithesis to the 'shaken, not stirred' Martini, jet-set world of James Bond, is not unaffected. In *Billion Dollar Brain*, Harry (Michael Caine) finds himself involved with a secret army financed by a Texan millionaire which, trying to invade Lithuania, comes to its end under the Baltic ice. It is an updated colour replay of a fourteenth-century battle on the ice between invading Teutonic Knights and native Russians portrayed in Sergei Eisenstein's Soviet film *Alexander Nevsky* (1938). The epic now echoes inside the recycled pleasures of kitsch.

James Bond, Harry Palmer: these cinema heroes were already figures of literary success. The spy story, after the detective story and science fiction, was the third genre generated by modern urban culture. While Bond maintained Britain's interests and the global status quo through asserting his manhood in various exotic locales, both Palmer and the embittered figures of John Le Carré's novels inhabited bleaker landscapes: 'that dangerous and sad city . . . which is the modern world' (Warshow, 1962).

The Ipcress File (National Film Archive, London)

Although the genre predates the Second World War (Conrad, Buchan), it is in the 1960s that it finally becomes established as a popular form in novels, cinema and TV. Meanwhile, spies in the real world had been fully integrated into the logic of 'pure war' (Virilio and Lotringer, 1983) – a total war that is undeclared and continued by other means: espionage, political assassination, surveillance, infiltration, destabilization. But while these methods are universal weapons, the spy story itself is very much a British affair. In a non-Oxbridge-educated world, where Empire and the pound sterling no longer offer reassurance, native authority and status become increasingly clandestine, secret. The drama of the spy, the revelation of this code, produces a privileged discourse on 'Britishness'. The tone may be cynical, chauvinistic or philosophically resigned, but it is around this cryptic abstraction that it tends to register.

Global stakes are frequently only public prizes in the deeper drama of betrayal and loss. For the betrayal, when it occurs, is not so much of

113

secrets (the Americans hold most of them anyway), but of an unwritten morality. It is the very act of betrayal that goes against the native grain, against 'being British'. The spy story is invariably the story of a moral style organized around loss: the loss of power, of status, of independence. The spy no longer symbolizes a confident, individual way of being, but a threatened and uncertain way of life. In this world, America as well as Russia is a menace; if US power is grudgingly accepted, its status is sarcastically lampooned: 'Walt Disney and Hollywood, Detroit and Madison Avenue . . . wrote the script for the American dream'. (Len Deighton, Billion Dollar Brain*)*

The first regular television broadcasting in the world was begun by the BBC in November 1936. But it was not until the mid-1950s and the arrival of commercial ITV broadcasting that we can begin to speak of popular television. It was ITV that pioneered popular television entertainment, introducing US shows like *I Love Lucy* and Police Sergeant Joe Friday in *Dragnet*, along with native quiz shows and variety: Hughie Green's *Double Your Money*, Michael Miles's *Take Your Pick*, and *Sunday Night at the London Palladium*. The BBC fought back with its own series or US counterparts: *Maigret*, *Dr Finlay's Casebook*, *Z Cars*, *Steptoe and Son*, *Perry Mason*; and with BBC 2 launched the historical romance format – *The Forsyte Saga*, *The Six Wives of Henry VIII*.

By the late '50s, both the BBC and ITV had discovered the popularity of TV reruns of old movies. There exists an under-40 film culture in Britain today, largely thanks to television. Cinema has become a celluloid archive, joining the magnetic memories of wax cylinders, records, tapes and cassettes. And many films, particularly foreign and avant-garde, obtained a far wider showing (usually late at night on BBC 2) than the cinema ever offered them.

But the principal organizing category in everyday television is 'light entertainment'. At peak viewing times this will involve *The . . . Show* format organized around a show-business personality, the 'star': Cilla Black, Tom Jones, Andy Williams, Lulu. Richard Dyer has suggested that such shows offer an 'aesthetics of escape'; an escape into a 'world in which necessity and scarcity have been defeated', but where the audience is also invited to participate in the domestication of the spectacle and have 'a good time' for the next forty-five minutes (Dyer, 1973). With their stable 'show biz' perspectives on sexuality, glamour and entertainment, these programmes offer a rather nostalgic style, further reflected in the very English props of 'Trad' jazz, and the hints of music hall and variety in the songs, the repartees, and the presence of stand-up comics. This is directly linked to a certain conception of their audience, to stable ideas about 'family entertainment'.

But the popular audience, the pleasures of 'the people' who regularly watch these and other programmes, remains the enigma inside the formula of 'entertainment'. The shifting form of the crime series represents another avenue into this universe. The change from the homely authority ('Evening all') of the local 'bobby' in *Dixon of Dock Green* to the post-'Dirty Harry' cynicism towards rules, law and authority in *The Sweeney* can be read, through the shifting dramatization of 'law and order', as a far more mobile sign in a certain style of television entertainment. It is not by chance that this shift is accompanied by a change in the focus of policing and crime and increasingly spectacular subjects: we move from the corner policeman and local station (Dock Green) through the policing of a town (*Z Cars*) to the 'war' against organized crime (the 'firm') in the metropolis.[5]

In these constructions of 'reality, that is the narrative you found yourself inheriting' (Hatton, 1985, 12), the fields of sense become complex, the issues more ambiguous. There are further twists in narrative conventions and representations: the Asian hero and anti-naturalism of *Gangsters*, the multi-layered sound-track and interweaving story-lines of *Hill Street Blues*, the female view of *Widows*.

Another, this time more stable, referent is that of the long-running 'soap opera'.[6] Here, across a relatively fixed ecology of principal characters and contexts, change and novelty tend to be charted by more transitory personalities.

Coronation Street, Britain's longest running serial, came out of the same moment as 'working-class realism' in British literature

The Clint Eastwood 'Dirty Harry' films in the early 1970s, together with The French Connection, *had an influence on the growing depiction of violence and cynicism towards authority on the part of police officers in subsequent British television series.*

and cinema (*Room At The Top, Saturday Night and Sunday Morning* etc.), the intellectual statement on that way of life: Richard Hoggart's *The Uses of Literacy*, and the cheeky pub humour of the 'Carry On' films. As Richard Dyer notes, the 'street' still remains caught up in that moment with its 'slice of life' representation of daily doings, gossip and relations (Dyer *et al.*, 1981). Marion Jordan makes the further point that its characters are, strictly speaking, rarely working-class (Dyer *et al.*, 1981). Yet it succeeds, through the half-light of rainy streets, grey brickwork, the smoky public bar and Northern accent, in projecting a view that is commonly understood to be 'working-class', or at least 'Hoggartsborough' (Reyner Banham).

(National Film Archive, London)

What all this actually represents today in the world of television and the context of contemporary popular culture is naturally more complex. The terms 'nostalgia' and 'romanticism', generated by an idea of a now deceased 'traditional' working-class community, might seem appropriate here. Part of the programme's subliminal charm and pleasure no doubt lies in

117

that direction, while its rootedness in the everyday exchange of gossip and comment across the bar and the shop counter, and in the front room, clearly distinguishes it from the very different contexts (and pleasures) of similar exchanges to be found in the wild excesses of money, style and power, in the American series *Dallas* and *Dynasty*.

Yet, on both sides of the Atlantic, in the down-to-earth accents of the British series, in the blunt kitsch of *Dallas* and the extravagant camp of *Dynasty*, we are constantly reminded that the programmes remain open in what they might represent. One of their most interesting dimensions has been their screening of sexuality. The more 'macho' *Dallas* tends to be limited here, but in *Dynasty*, Steve Carrington is shown to be gay, while Elsie Tanner (*Coronation Street*) and Alexis Carrington (*Dynasty*) have publicly opened up a space usually denied to women before: the 'sexualization of the middle-aged', and with it, 'an important extension of the range of imagery which is offered to women in popular forms' (Lovell, in Dyer *et al.*, 1981, 52). These images, like those of the earlier film noir, and Gainsborough melodrama, represent an important overspill from more conventional forms, producing a contradictory and ambiguous relation to the previous limits of the 'normal'.[7]

. . . inside the machine

What is initially so striking about the world of photography, cinema and television, is that they appear, as the Italian film director Pier Paolo Pasolini once put it, to 'represent reality with reality', to use a 'system of signs which coincide with the system of signs of reality' (Stack, 1969). The visual media do 'appear' to operate in this manner. Yet, despite their 'natural' properties, they are not simply 'reflections' of the world, but transforming activities in it. They mediate and participate in our experiences, our sense of the everyday, our knowledge, our culture (Fiske and Hartley, 1978, 161). This has inevitably forced a shift in perspectives, in the contemporary eye, in 'reality'.

Set against the gloomy predictions of a media-induced

> **'Our era' does not prefer images to real things out of perversity but partly in response to the ways in which the notion of what is real has been progressively complicated and weakened.** (Sontag, 1979a)

totalitarianism, however, there is the daily, inventive, evidence of local control, local meanings and a continual construction of sense that passes beyond the instrumental logic of the 'culture industry'. It is probably not by chance that it is in Britain, the first country to experience industrialism, mass urbanization and the development of a popular urban commercial culture, that the domestic ownership of video recorders and home computers is amongst the highest in the world. The discovery of personal spaces *inside* the media, on the other side of the screen, as it were, occurs after a lengthy habit of 'tactile appropriation' (Walter Benjamin).

The images of our world are increasingly transitory. The information they convey is rapidly consumed. Their circulation is correspondingly forced to accelerate. The video clip attempts simultaneously to connect a particular sound with the immediate languages of contemporary youth culture (fashion, dance, romance, style, graphic art, advertising), linking the pulse of the music to the wider rhythms of an increasingly 'international leisure style' (Paul Rambali). The time between receiving and processing the image is progressively eliminated. We view screens that are filled with 'flashing, darting electronic signifiers' (Fiske and Watts, 1985).

Involved here is not only the technological invasion of our imagination but also a new order of sense. In the interface between the viewing machines and the programmes, there are hands on the TV controls, the joystick or the keyboard. In the interface between hard- and software is a socialized cultural-ware. The 'machines produce messages but no meanings, thus leaving a semiotic space for the player to become author' (Fiske and Watts, 1985). The programmes themselves can be personalized and re-written.

119

The technology of reproduction – television and cassette players, VCRs, Walkmans and computers – raises the question of who 'owns' the image, sound or programme. The hardware puts into the hands of many the potential for making and combining fresh sounds, images and languages. Programmes recorded off the TV can be edited, mixed and recombined in a second moment ('time-shifting') to produce a novel audio–visual montage or 'scratch video' such as the Duvet Brothers' 'Blue

120

Monday': 'the individual talks back to television' (Gorilla Tapes Group). Personalized programmes, viewing and listening habits are continually assembled by using the fast-forward and reverse buttons on the VCR and cassette player, or by writing individual computer programs in BASIC or PASCAL. Here we

enter the machine, recognize the codes, and begin to manipulate the languages.

Across the screen, imagery and sound is re-presented, re-cycled, re-written. The unity of a single point of view – that of the writer, the director, the medium – is mediated, modified, sometimes contested. The programmes themselves are involuntarily inserted into everyday networks that suggest further connections and meanings. Moments of pleasure when watching a film, playing a video game or following a TV serial represent transitory instances of attention in the distractedly absorbed montage of the present.

We will return to this idea of an urban collage in the Conclusions; let us now turn to the popular soundtrack that has accompanied some of these developments.

Notes

1. Even restricting our attention to a vague categorization of popular cinema and television since 1945, we can see that the output of material and comment is vast. The itinerary I have followed here has been conditioned both by the significance of certain examples and by recent commentary. For example, suggestive analyses of film noir, Gainsborough costumed melodrama, television light entertainment and 'soap opera', all influenced by questions of sexual typing, feminism and the detailed possibilities of everyday popular culture, have appeared in the last few years. I have drawn extensively on this work. See References for details.

2. The real culprit here is not so much Hollywood as British 'naturalism'. It is, above all, this native strain that draws upon the nineteenth-century novel and a realism based on 'an empirical notion of truth': 'The camera shows us what happens – it tells the truth against which we can measure the discourses' (MacCabe, 1981).

3. For further details and interpretations of these films, see Kaplan (1980).

4. See Sontag (1979b) and Core (1984).

5. For further details see the issue on 'The Sweeney', *Screen Education*, 20, 1976.

6. The term 'soap' arises from the fact that US daytime shows, aimed at a housewife public, were pioneered with the sponsorship of soap manufacturers. In this sense, neither *Coronation Street* nor *Dynasty* are strictly 'soap'. Their evening audiences are more heterogeneous than the house-bound wife and mother.

7. This argument clearly relates to possible feminist readings of melodrama and the 'gendered audience' that watches them. We have already encountered this possibility with film noir and Gainsborough Gothic. For a further discussion on this in the context of television, see Dyer *et al.* (1981), and *Screen*, vol. 25, 1, 1984 which is devoted to this argument.

Suggestions for further work

1. There is a fundamental difference between a reproduced painting and a duplicated photograph that marks the end of a certain social and aesthetic control of the image. Try and explain why.

2. **I saw *Shane* in Tokyo with a Japanese friend. All the audience cried. The next evening I went home taking the elevated railway that surrounds the city centre like the Chicago Loop, and which passes behind the cinema where they were showing *Shane*. Well, from the carriage of the train I heard a character in the film: the child at the end calling Alan Ladd 'Shane, Shane, come back'. That for me is the symbol of the cultural domination of Hollywood: the voice of America in a calm summer night in a city in the Far East.** (Angela Carter, *La Repubblica*, 20/10/84)

Having read this chapter and the preceding one, think of ways of explaining what the 'cultural domination of Hollywood' implies. Try and point out how this domination is not simply imposed by big money and giant corporations taking decisions in California, but also responds to popular tastes in a way that traditional and local forms and institutions often seem unable to do. You will find it useful to think of cinema as a new and accessible language that encounters resistance from older institutions (literature and theatre, for example), and to point to the examples given in various places in this book of how Hollywood film has frequently suggested a possible style and image for local concerns in dress, pleasure, sexuality and the imaginary.

3. You seemingly just point the camera and 'capture' a shot from the surrounding world. What is actually coded – the choice of shot, subject, angle, camera, film, exposure, lens, speed, and eventual development, emphasis, cut, montage – passes as 'natural': a 'message without a code' (Roland Barthes). Think of why the assumption that the powers of the image can offer us direct contact with what is happening in front of the camera, with 'reality', has given rise to different forms of 'realism'. Illustrate this by referring to the distinct visions offered by Hollywood and by British cinema, magazines and television.

4. British naturalism has proved to offer some particularly powerful views of social reality in its various documentary forms. At the same time, important details in that reality remain unobserved. Give some examples of this blindness and explain why they occur.

5. Clearly there was more than one type of cinema available to the British public in the major period of cinema-going (1930s–1950s). Apart from the obvious national distinction between American and British film there were further, internal, differences. The same was also the case with the 'private' entertainment supplied by television after the 1950s. Try to identify some of the genres that have proved popular and see if you can offer some explanation for their popularity and the potential meanings they have suggested.

6. The increasing presence of media technology in the home and public places – from television and the video recorder to the arcade game and the computer – has fuelled the pessimism of those commentators and critics who see in it only further evidence of a 'controlled' culture and 'programmed' tastes. Think of arguments to counter this by developing and extending Susan Sontag's idea that the 'subsequent industrialisation of camera technology only carried out a promise inherent in photography from its very beginnings: to democratise all experiences by translating them into images' (Sontag, 1979a, 7).

(David Johnson)

PART THREE
THE SOUNDS

7 FROM MUSIC HALL TO HITSVILLE

Popular music, pop music: from the radio, in the music hall, off the screen, on the juke box, on the record player, in the dance hall, at the club, in youth cultures, in the street . . . urban sounds, the sounds of our time. The activities surrounding popular music, and the place it occupies in the often distractedly received soundscape of the contemporary city, suggests, despite the 'noise' and 'nonsense' regularly attributed to it, that it involves an intelligible soundtrack. In the next three chapters I will try to indicate where some of these sounds came from and what some of them might 'mean'.

September 1984

September 1984, and I am looking at the cover of *New Musical Express*. It consists of a large colour photograph of James Brown and Afrika Bambaataa. James Brown smiles into the camera. 'Bam', with a mohican crop, hides behind the lattice pattern of his grille-style shades. A meeting of different generations of black music. James Brown, now well into his fifties, is the 'Godfather of Soul', the man who never went away. Afrika Bambaataa is the young prophet of black culture from the Bronx, where electro-funk and rap, graffiti and break-dancing are creating the sounds, shapes and sentiments of 'hip hop'.

The fact that James Brown and Afrika Bambaataa are making

129

a record ('Unity') together in New York should be of such interest to one of Britain's leading pop music papers is of course significant. It suggests that events in New York, at least on the musical front, have an *immediate* relevance to the readers of *NME*.

This American connection, as we have already seen elsewhere, is not of recent origin. In fact, in British popular music, even before the music hall, a 'transatlantic idiom' was already present with the blacked-up American troupes of Nigger Minstrels and 'coon' singers in the early nineteenth century. In their wake the voice of America found its way into the music hall and British popular culture and variety, steadily growing in volume, from the 1840s onwards.

If the later intrusion of Hollywood, American dance crazes and music has seemed merely to reflect US economic and cultural power in the twentieth-century world, the earlier proximity of American music and popular culture to that of British entertainment was actually established across common musical, linguistic and commercial structures. It was in these two countries, where different cultural and geographical conditions were counterbalanced by a shared economic wealth, language, and the new exigencies of massive urbanization, that commercial leisure industries were pioneered. The subsequent weight of US popular entertainment in this equation is undeniable.

On the boards

In the 1880s, London had more than 500 music halls where names and fortunes were being made. However, their right to exist was frequently challenged. The drink, the noise, the smoke, the excitement, the whistles and cat-calls when the artist 'got the bird', led many 'respectable' commentators to consider the halls regular dens of vice. Colin MacInnes refers to 'the subversive Music Hall tradition', a slightly cynical worm's-eye view of the world where the upper-class 'swells' and 'toffs' of the West End, the 'Champagne Charlies' and 'Burlington Berties', were mercilessly lampooned (MacInnes, 1969).

In 1878, an Act of Parliament was passed imposing stricter legislation on the halls. Many were forced to close. By the end of the century, even before the threat of cinema and records had been appreciated, the halls were retreating into the increasingly nostalgic, occasionally jingoistic, twilight of respectability.

The music hall initially grew up as an extension of the pub, laying on food (pigs' trotters and pease pudding were popular) and entertainment. Amongst the first was Charles Morton's Canterbury Arms in the late 1840s. But by the 1890s music halls were being built as separate establishments. It was in the Palace in Shaftesbury Avenue, built by the same Charles Morton; the Metropolitan, Edgware Road; the Granville, Waltham Green; the Bedford, Camden Town; and the Old Mogul, Drury Lane; that Marie Lloyd, already a star at sixteen, sang such hits as 'A little of what you fancy does you good', 'Knocked 'em out in the Old Kent Road', 'Oh, Mr Porter', 'My old man says, "Follow the van"'.

Those who found success in the halls – Marie Lloyd, Dan Leno, Vesta Tilley (who specialized in male impersonations: 'Burlington Bertie'), Albert Chevalier – often made (and spent) fortunes. Many performers earned more than a £100 a week. They toured outside London and abroad, in Australia and the United States. Charlie Chaplin and Stan Laurel first visited the USA with Fred Karno's Krazy Komics – a music hall act. They were stars, usually of proletarian origins, and were expected to live in an exaggerated style of 'winkles and champagne'. When Marie Lloyd died in 1922, aged 52: 'the taps on the bars around Leicester Square were draped in black, and 100,000 Londoners watched the coffin leave her house in Golders Green' (MacInnes, 1969, 38–9).

The songs – 'I'm Henerey the Eighth, I am', 'All the nice girls love a sailor', 'Any Old Iron?', 'Boiled Beef and Carrots' – with their researched Cockney aura of 'dropped aitches and fings' were written by professional songwriters and rarely by the performers themselves. And by the 1880s, British popular music, dominated by London money, tastes and stars, was a thoroughly commercial enterprise. It was to the London halls that artists in search of success migrated, not only from the provinces (George Formby Senior), but also from Australia: from Melbourne Albert Whelan and Florrie Forde ('Pack up your troubles in your old kit bag', 'Down at the old Bull and Bush'). Supported by a large paying public and supplied with music and performers by professional songwriters and impresarios (by the end of the century a chain of 'Empire' halls had been built around the country), urban popular music had become a thoroughly commercialized pleasure.

The coming of the record

The commercialization of music making was initially due to the introduction of industry in the form of the printing press.

James Catnach, who set up as a printer of street literature in Monmouth Court, Seven Dials, in 1814, is said to have paid men to collect ballads from singers in country taverns. (Lloyd, 1975, 27)

Later, there would be the even more rapid means of electronic transmission: records, radio, film, television, video. But both extremes of *musical reproduction* – nineteenth-century song sheets and piano rolls or contemporary digital recording and video discs – offer the prospect of an increasing access to a common soundscape: a nationally organized, tendentially cosmopolitan, popular music.

Despite the rowdy success of the Victorian music hall, and perhaps because of it, the popular music industry was also built on the more respectable growth of private entertainment; often the only space accessible to Victorian women. It was the presence first of the piano and then of the gramophone and the wireless, both in the middle–class drawing room and in the working–class parlour, that provided much of its 'mass' audience and market.

The record player – first called the phonograph – was invented by the American, Thomas Edison, in 1877. Until the mid-1920s, recordings were made mechanically: a needle cutting a wax cylinder or flat disc. After 1898 phonographs and cylinders became commercially available in Britain. In the next decade discs appeared and millions of cylinders were being sold annually. All types of music – music hall, operatic arias, revue, rags, folk, novelty – were recorded. By 1928 it was estimated that there were more than 2½ million record players in Britain (Hustwitt, 1983, 6–7). In the following decade, after the shake out of the economic crash in 1929 and the Depression, EMI and Decca emerged as the two major British record companies. They were to dominate the home market until the mid-1950s.

Tin Pan Alley

But although the record industry was growing and the circuits of sound reproduction were soon to be dramatically expanded by the introduction of radio, the basis of the music industry in the early twentieth century was professional song writing: 'Tin Pan Alley'. Before there were royalties from the sales of records and fees paid each time a record was played, songwriters and music publishers made their money through sheet music sales. The hits of the day, particularly after the decline of music hall, came from here. In Britain's case this meant London, usually Denmark Street.

In order to reach the public, professional 'pluggers' were sent out to persuade famous stars to adopt the songs. Those who accepted were naturally recompensed. These operations were quite blatant. 'Yes, we have no bananas', the rage of 1923. involved many hands in Tin Pan Alley and quoted numerous tunes; it was then 'plugged' and promoted until it became a 'hit'. It was a clear indication of the new realities in cultural production that had been established, at least in Britain and the United States, by the early twentieth century.

American liberties

These tendencies were further accelerated in the traumatic years

133

and aftermath of the First World War. British commercial popular music – music hall and its paler aftermath, 'variety' – was challenged and usurped by 'ragtime', 'jazz' and an enthusiasm for dance steps that came from the other side of the Atlantic: the Argentinian tango, but above all, the North American 'animal dances' – the Foxtrot, the Buzzard Lope, the Bunny Hug. These dances were both simpler than the European dances they replaced and allowed greater body movement. They also permitted more freedom for women to take the initiative in dancing patterns; they no longer had to be 'led' by the men around the dance floor.

In popular music, dancing is the fundamental connection between the pleasures of sound and their social realization in the libidinal movement of bodies, styles and sensual forms. It represents a social encounter, which can be a dance hall, a club, or a party, where bodies are permitted to respond to physical rhythms that elsewhere would not be tolerated; the moment when romanticism brushes against reality, and a transitory step out of the everyday can be enjoyed. For women and youth in the early decades of this century it promised that there existed something more beyond the rules and routines they were normally expected to carry.

The popularity of public dancing was such that hotels and restaurants, imitating a pattern already established in New York, began providing ballrooms and dancing areas. This, in turn, encouraged the growth of professional dance bands. Dancing was detached from its early association with drink, prostitution, rowdyism, fights and other 'low life' habits. In the 1920s, we find dance music coming from London's West End hotels, with band leaders dressed in tails playing to the idle rich at the Savoy Hotel, the Dorchester, Grosvenor House, and the Mayfair.

But dancing was above all a popular pleasure. In the glittering decor of The Hammersmith Palais de Danse (opened in 1919), the Streatham Locarno, the Astoria in Charing Cross Road, and literally hundreds of dance halls around the country, every night thousands danced the Foxtrot, the Charleston and the Shimmy to the music of The Versatile Rag Pickers, The American Five, and The Original Dixieland Jazz Band.

The lack of propriety in bodily movements that the undisciplined steps and wild sounds of 'jazz' apparently unleashed were gradually eradicated by a growing army of dance instructors led by Victor Sylvester, and the increasingly predictable metronome

rhythms of the white dance bands.[1] What jazz might have been about was flattened beneath the dancing master's shoes and the band leader's baton to an acceptable dance hall decorum.

Meanwhile, despite its exclusive atmosphere, the dance music being played in the West End hotels was also managing to reach a vast audience. In 1923, the BBC began broadcasting it, and, as radio ownership expanded through the 1920s, rolling up the carpet and dancing at home to West End orchestras became something of a national institution.

By 1933, a pattern of late-night dance music (so-called) had clearly emerged. Monday through Friday, from ten-thirty until midnight, you could hear, at the flip of a

switch, Sydney Lipton from the Grosvenor House, Jack Johnson from the Dorchester, Carroll Gibbons from the Savoy, and Lew Stone from the Monseigneur. And on Saturday nights, the most glittering prize the air waves could afford – Ambrose and his Orchestra from the Mayfair. (Colin, 1977, 34)

Alongside the success of US-derived dance music was the rise of the solo singer or 'crooner'. The individual emotionalism of the crooning style – 'the world of the private nightmare', as Richard Hoggart once acidly described it – was again of American origin. Rudy Vallee and Bing Crosby were the famous initiators, and later Frank Sinatra the most acclaimed practitioner. In Britain there was Denny Dennis, Al Bowlly, Peggy Dell and Evelyn Dall. Anglicized tones were maintained by the more restrained 'Englishness' of the British dance bands and the singing of Gracie Fields and a little later by Vera Lynn (the 'Forces' sweetheart'). But undoubtedly the most influential image amongst these new musical styles was that provided by Hollywood in the 1930s with the arrival of sound film and the musical.

Ironically enough the triumph of the American musical represented the condensation of the whole European 'light' music tradition, which in the late nineteenth and early twentieth centuries had developed from opera into operetta (for example, *The Merry Widow*), and then into the revue and the show.

The success of Broadway musicals – *Show Boat, Porgy and Bess, Oklahoma!*, with songs and music from Cole Porter, George Gershwin, Rodgers and Hart, Jerome Kern – and their subsequent Hollywood translation and transmission, drove a further nail into the coffin of British variety. These films provided an insight into another world: a world of relaxed male singers, elegant dancing, smooth sounds and stylized glamour. European formalities – tails, gowns, walking sticks and top hats – were transformed into 'possible props for an improvised ballet' (Michael Wood in Feuer, 1982); a fantastic and seductive transatlantic imagery: Fred Astaire and Ginger Rogers in *Top Hat, Swing Time, Flying Down To Rio*.

137

By the end of the 1930s, the Hollywood studios had moved decisively into the music business and owned most of the music publishing in Tin Pan Alley. The control of popular music now apparently lay in a few hands. The German philosopher and music critic, Theodor Adorno, then resident in the United States, talked of a standardized sound being distractedly consumed each day like a cigarette or a bowl of corn flakes. Yet, despite its powers, Hollywood show business discovered only a momentary success in its attempt to manage the sounds and voices of popular pleasure. By the early 1940s, its empire was already tottering.

Notes

1. In 1924, The Imperial Society of Dance Teachers codified ballroom dancing and decreed that dancing should confine itself to four basic steps: the waltz, the foxtrot, the quick-step and the tango. Forming his own band to provide these strict dance tempi, Victor Sylvester went on to sell more than 27 million records.

8 OTHER SOUNDS, OTHER WORLDS

Another America

Beyond the New York–Hollywood world of Tin Pan Alley, Broadway shows, musicals, crooners and radio stars, there existed the rest of America. There was white folk or 'hillbilly' music. There was also the even more obscure world of black music, of jazz, of the blues.

In distant Britain, the distinction between white dance music and much of jazz was also maintained. Jazz was excluded from the BBC. Duke Ellington toured in 1933 and Louis Armstrong in 1935, but their concerts were poorly attended. The only public point of local reference for British jazz enthusiasts was the musical paper *Melody Maker*. In Soho night clubs and bottle parties in the '30s, a small jazz band scene developed in after-hours jam sessions. It was to clubs like The Bag of Nails, The Manhattan, The Bat Club, The Nut House, The Nest, that visiting black jazz musicians – Louis Armstrong, Coleman Hawkins, members of Duke Ellington's band – would drop in (Colin, 1977).

But this music remained hidden, not only and more obviously in Britain, but also in the United States. It was only after translation into the subdued rhythms and tones of white dance music under the guidance of such band leaders as the aptly named Paul Whiteman that the resulting music received a more extensive hearing.

Nevertheless, as the transmission of music grew with the spread of records and radio, it became increasingly difficult to block access to Afro-American music. The phenomenal success of Benny Goodman in 1935 was largely due to radio hook-up but the basis of the music, its innovative appeal and freshness, lay in the hands of arranger Fletcher Henderson and the black jazz band tradition he represented. And although Tin Pan Alley came up with its own, 'sweeter', version of swing – Glen Miller and 'Moonlight Serenade' – the sounds of change were increasingly in the air.

Hollywood meanwhile, owning most of the publishing rights on popular music, decided in the early 1940s to squeeze more revenues from the music being played on the radio. The radio stations retaliated by setting up their own publishing company. Forced to look outside Tin Pan Alley for their material, the previously segregated minority sounds of country and black music were discovered and slowly, but irreversibly, found a space on the radio.

At first, it was the music of the white, rural south that attained a wider hearing. The isolated regional life styles, earlier symbolized in the lonesome yodel of Jimmie Rodgers, received a further romantic twist when, in the 1940s, country music entered American Destiny (and Hollywood) and re-emerged in cowboy clothes and sentiments as 'country and western': Roy Acuff, Gene Autry. But country music, almost in spite of its bland morality, also hinted at previously hidden margins: where innocence and experience co-existed in the same troubled soul, where Hank Williams, aged 29, dies on the back seat of one of his five Cadillacs after a lifetime of country music, booze and pills. A road followed a quarter of a century later by another country boy, Elvis Aaron Presley.

As the thirties dissolved into the forties and the cataclysm of the Second World War, and American soldiers arrived in Britain equipped with 'V-discs' of swing music given away free to the GIs by the US government, the public triumph of big bands (Benny Goodman, Artie Shaw, Woody Herman) and crooners (Bing Crosby, Frank Sinatra) was increasingly accompanied by the distant sounds of other musics: Duke Ellington, Count Basie, the blues and jazz of Afro-America.

In the restless night: black America

Afro-American music, the forced marriage of Europe and Africa in the Americas, had already provided popular urban music with sounds and ideas since the early 1800s. The gross mimicry of the supposed music and mannerisms of black people in black-face 'minstrels' and 'coon' singers had been a regular part of British music hall entertainment. There had also been the public success of spirituals, this time sung by black men and women. The all-black Fisk University Jubilee Singers had a successful British tour in 1871 with such songs as 'Swing Low Sweet Chariot' and 'Nobody Knows The Trouble I've Seen' (Lee, 1982, 81).

The cultural inheritance of slavery and the daily experience of racism turned black music into a loaded manifesto. Black rhythms in a white world formed a cultural counterpoint that frequently elided, resisted and refused the labels of white imposition. So, the Cakewalk – the dance rage of 'high society' in the first decade of this century – was the direct descendant of the plantation dances of the slaves that, in the words of the son of a former slave, parodied 'the high manners of the white folks in the "big house", but their masters, who gathered round to watch the fun, missed the point' (in Shepherd, 1982, 18).

It was ragtime, originally a black piano style whose most famous practitioner had been Scott Joplin, that became, together with dancing the Cakewalk, the first of many Afro-American styles to stretch out from the commercial music centre of New York to the farthest corners of the world.

Ragtime, as John Shepherd points out, involved the meeting of Europe and Africa between the hands on the piano.

The left hand of piano ragtime plays in a very regular . . . rhythm typical of European music. The right hand, however, plays in what is known as 'syncopated' fashion . . . . The notes of the right hand (the melody) seem to 'cut across' those of the left hand (the bass line), and it is this

141

'cutting across' which makes ragtime tunes seem so catchy. (Shepherd, 1982, 27)

Once adopted by Tin Pan Alley, ragtime was simplified and the syncopation abandoned. It was speeded up to become 'wild' and 'flashy', and then achieved massive success in such numbers as Irving Berlin's 'Alexander's Ragtime Band' (1911). Tin Pan Alley, however, was only an outlet for white songs. So, despite the success of ragtime, racial segregation in the entertainment world continued – there was white vaudeville and black vaudeville, each with their separate booking agencies.

Between the wars, black music remained largely hidden away in the 'race' catalogues of the record companies. It was certainly not heard on the radio or in the dance halls. Black music was largely restricted to a black audience in bars and 'jukes' along the highway, fish fries and picnics in the country, house rent parties in the city ghettoes and, in the case of gospel music, to the black church. For the more famous there were vaudeville shows, punishing cross-country tours, and the dim-lit world of night clubs, to arrive finally in Chicago or at the legendary Cotton Club in Harlem and the white bohemia and criminal underworld that hovered around its sounds.

If the music of King Oliver, Louis Armstrong, Duke Ellington and Fletcher Henderson had first to be 'bleached' and presented by white musicians before it was considered suitable for distribution by the radio, record companies and booking agencies, then it was hardly surprising that their untutored musical source – the blues – was almost completely ignored. Although the term 'blues', like 'rag' and 'jazz', was almost obligatory in the repertory of dance band pieces in the 1920s and 1930s, it usually represented only a distant echo of Afro-America. The moaned sentiments of Bessie Smith, the powerful barrelhouse or 'boogie-woogie' piano style of Jimmy Yancey, the penetrating voices and disturbing guitar patterns (often created by using a knife or bottleneck on the strings) of Blind Lemon Jefferson and Robert Johnson, the powerful blues-based jazz of Count Basie, Lester Young and Jimmy Rushing that came out of the Midwest from Kansas City, the melancholy

142

notes of Billie Holliday, all arrived literally from another world.

The long absorption of black sounds into white dance music, the break-up of Tin Pan Alley's monopoly on music publishing and radio music, and the accelerated cultural effects of wartime living (in particular, the black migration into Northern industries), did mean, however, that the subterranean traditions of Afro-American music became more public after 1940. Black music began to appear on the radio: 'It was impossible to segregate the airwaves' (Chapple and Garofalo, 1977, 30). The term 'Rhythm and Blues' replaced the offensive limitations of 'race' music as radio and records carried this music to new ears. Meanwhile, with growing public exposure, gospel and R&B increasingly crossed each other's paths before finally joining in soul music. Gospel harmony or the lone, smoky voice, honking saxophones or a wistful tenor, electric guitars, insistent cross-rhythms and a deep-running bass: this was the indigo universe of Charlie Parker, Mahalia Jackson, Joe Turner, Fats Domino, T-Bone Walker, Muddy Waters, Howlin' Wolf, B. B. King, Bo Diddley, Ray Charles, Sam Cooke . . . the sounds of a once obscured body: the 'blues people'.

Despite its apparent connnection to white dance and music labels ('jazz', 'swing', 'blues'), it was the very separatedness of

black music, at least outside the South where it continually overspilled into white country music, that produced an exotic difference – with all the subsequent attractions and rejections. After the 1940s, this sonorial tension, this continual passage between black and white, was to become the driving force behind the majority of developments in popular music.

It had already been revealingly prefigured in the select interchange between black 'bebop' and white hipsters during and after the Second World War. Bebop was an approach to playing jazz pioneered by black musicians in New York in the early 1940s. In the playing of Charlie Parker, Thelonious Monk, Kenny Clarke, Dizzy Gillespie, Charlie Christian, and a young Miles Davis, we hear the inheritance of the blues: in both the rhythm and the harmonic frame there is a shift away from the older jazz practice of improvising on the melody to digging underneath it and improvising on the chords on which the melody is based. This rhythmic and harmonic flexibility opened up a new freedom: 'we used to talk our way through the melody, very fast, just chattering away with anything that came into our heads' (Dizzy Gillespie in Palmer, 1977, 62).

Around this select black urban music, white bohemia drew out some significant connections in the romantic figure of the 'hipster': zoot-suited, smoking marijuana, and 'jive-talking' with all the other 'hep-cats' in the American night.[1] But there was also the other side of 'bebop': an artistic and cultural isolation, heightened by drugs (particularly heroin), a hermeneutic language and style, which for the black boppers was also a self-conscious comment on their position in white America. Bebop, like the 'free' jazz of John Coltrane and Ornette Coleman fifteen years later, was considered by white music critics, on America's *Downbeat* and Britain's *Melody Maker*, to be 'anti-jazz', an insult to *their* taste . . . which, of course, was what was intended.

The heart of Afro-American music is improvising, that is, making use of what is available and translating it into a particular voice, sound, cultural statement. We can hear this in bebop and we can hear it in rap, in dub and in scratch: an extension of the tradition of subverting the languages of the white Master. The musical syntax of the blues, of gospel, of jazz, R&B, bebop, and soul, shifted emphasis away from European melody to a feeling ('soul', 'funk') for the vertical interiors of sound and pitch. Attention is switched to working 'inside' the tune, bending and stretching the notes and rhythms. Structures are subverted by feel, linear developments sacrificed to a body of sound. Here lies the difference between the 'black stream' and the mainstream (Larry Coleman).

And where gospel and reggae lyrics have appropriated the language of the Bible for black redemption, rap, scratch and dub have subsequently extended this strategy to conquering the electronic speech of the urban media. The microphone and the record turntable become musical instruments, direct extensions of a black urban grammar. Records are mixed and 'scratched' together, producing new sounds each time they are played, producing open texts and new, local powers. This is what Imamu Baraka (LeRoi Jones) has called the perpetual 'contemporaneity' of black music: its continual drawing upon the changing social and cultural currents of the moment to produce a metalanguage of experience, of resistance, of everyday life (LeRoi Jones, 1963).

By the 1950s, blue lines were spreading irreversibly over the map of white popular music. Blue notes on the radio were widening musical tastes. And rhythm – explicit in bebop, in R&B, in the simple insistence of rock'n'roll – was becoming a priority.

Reaction, revival, and renewal: 'folk' musics

Such twentieth-century developments in popular music as its commercial organization in Tin Pan Alley, its mass distribution through records and radio, and the clear domination of American song and dance styles, have provoked a series of reactions and 'revivals'.

These responses to the commercialization, and its frequently employed synonym, the Americanization, of popular music looked to the solid assurance of roots; looked to the presumably more 'authentic' sounds of popular culture before it was invaded, organized and contaminated by commerce and the dictates of the market place. This periodic turning to folk music has also been indirectly supported by popular musical critics regularly calling for authentic sounds to be set against the commercial din of the pop music world.[2]

The English folk-song revival that began in the early years of the twentieth century, widely associated with the folk-song collector Cecil Sharpe and the interest of certain classical composers such as Percy Grainger and Vaughan Williams, was clearly part of the far wider reaction to industrial life, urbanization, commercial pleasure, and the passing away of an increasingly idealized 'olde England'. Like the then contemporary Arts and Crafts Movement, the cottage model and garden city in domestic architecture, the folk-song movement formed part of a persuasive rural vision. And although frequently radical, it was not untouched by deeply conservative sentiments when it set its face against the city and defended the hazy 'folk' traditions of another 'England'. In the context of what by 1900 was an overwhelmingly literate and urban popular culture, it was a self-conscious act of conservation, carried out in the name of a 'people' who were quite frankly elsewhere.

Sixty years later, during another folk revival, the folk music historian A. L. Lloyd praised white youth for returning to folk song and rejecting the 'frenzied despair of the Rolling Stones and their go-go-go successors' (Lloyd, 1975, 371). Yet, the idea that fresh-faced university students singing of daggers, roses and graves should somehow be expressing something more 'authentic' than other pale, though far less healthy looking, youths singing electrically amplified blues, seems mere intellectual conceit.

The despised music of the Rolling Stones and the other British R&B groups of the early 1960s was also born out of the ashes of a revival as fervent as the English folk-song movement, that of Trad jazz. Both the folk and Trad booms resonated with ambivalence, for the reverse side of revival is renovation. The second time round, such musics need not automatically signify nostalgia; they can suggest new directions.

White folk music, much of it retraced and preserved in the

eastern mountain states of the USA, was not simply of antiquarian interest. When it re-emerged in the 1960s, first in the folk clubs and later in the charts, it also represented a novel sound. With its literate qualities and simple musical accompaniment it proved particularly attractive to the educated children of the middle classes. It also provided a new and an accessible entrance to pop.[3] Donovan, following the style of Bob Dylan, first appeared on *Ready, Steady, Go!* in 1965 without a Vox amplifier and a Fender; just an acoustic guitar and a harmonica were enough to make him a star. And after the triumph of British beat music and R&B, folk often seemed the only avenue, apart from show business, left open to white women wishing to

The banner of 'authentic' music has been raised several times in recent decades: in the 1940s and '50s with Trad jazz, in the '60s with the second folk revival, and in the late '60s and early '70s with white rock's criticisms of contemporary black music. In all these cases, white audiences rediscover yesterday's blues, 'authentic' sounds that have evaded the corruption of commerce and the city. What is most striking in all these cases is how a white regard for past, often black, musics (rural blues, Trad jazz, and the distillation of rural sounds – C&W, the blues, and white folk music – in the anti-urbanism of the 1960s counterculture) finds itself contesting novel and flexible developments in urban black music: bebop, R&B, soul, Motown, reggae, disco; that is, finds itself contesting black modernism and its investigation of contemporary authenticities (i.e. 'where things are at').

enter the male empire of pop music in the mid and late 1960s.

The hermetic conservatism of revivalism was equally important in the emergence of Trad jazz in the 1940s. Again, it was the work of dividing 'false' sounds from 'authentic' jazz that inspired an almost messianic fervour. Oblivious of bebop and the booming blues of Kansas City jazz, the white revivalists insisted that true jazz only existed in the sounds of 20–30 years previously. The music of the Ken Coyler band sought the purity of a New Orleans sound circa 1910 and, if less fanatical in their approach, the rest of the British Trad following was devoted to ignoring the 'modernists' (who could range from Louis Armstrong's Hot Five of the 1920s to contemporary bebop), evaluating obscure musicians of yesteryear and discussing the matrix numbers of long-deleted records, issued by now defunct record companies.

Once again, resistance to the present nurtured innovation: this time in white bohemia. While the finger-snapping beats of Jack Kerouac's generation picked contemporary jazz to accompany their existential journey 'on the road' into America –

... performing our one and noble function of the time, *move*. And we moved! We flashed past the mysterious white signs in the night somewhere in New Jersey that say SOUTH (with an arrow) and WEST (with an arrow) and took the south one. New Orleans! It burned in our brains. (Kerouac, 1958, 133–4)

– the British variant of the 1950s was inevitably far more homely. The domestic mixture of New Orleans jazz with cups of tea, warm beer and lawn-mowed suburbia rarely pushed British bohemia towards the intellectual spirituality of modernism and movement.

There were exceptions, particularly in the visual arts; and the rise of the British Pop Art movement, where artists such as Eduardo Paolozzi, Richard Hamilton and David Hockney, and critics Lawrence Alloway and Reyner Banham, boldly sketched out a new aesthetics that renovated modernism with the impact of popular culture and its tastes. But the bohemia that hovered

148

around the jazz clubs – the 'beatniks' identified by the popular press on the Aldermaston CND marches ('Ban the Bomb') – usually opted for the decidedly more English route of eccentric dress and manners.

. . . an extreme sloppiness was *de rigueur* both on stage and off. The duffle coat was a cult object, sandals with socks a popular if repulsive fad, beards common, and bits of battle dress, often dyed navy blue, almost a uniform. The source of this was largely the post-war art schools. (Melly, 1970, 19–20)

A decade later, sloppiness and a passion for musical exotica was to pass through and out of the art schools and jazz clubs into the wider stream of pop music. The 100 Club, Oxford Street, once the home of the London Jazz Society, became an R&B club and then, acquiring an altogether sharper style, a mod soul venue.

Notes

1. For a vivid account of black Harlem hip-dom in the early 1940s, and the 'groovy, frantic scenes in different chicks' and cats' pads, where with the lights down mellow, everybody blew gage and juiced back and jumped', *The Autobiography of Malcolm X* (1968) is essential reading. As a retrospective view of Malcolm's own hustling hip youth as 'Detroit Red' before being imprisoned and converted to Islam, its moralism disperses much of the white romanticism that hangs around black street life and styles.
2. As, for example, in the mid-1950s when the British musical press set the folk-music qualities of rural blues against contemporary urban electric blues and their uncomfortable affinity with the 'tasteless' sounds of rock'n'roll, see Chambers (1985). For a later, and equally important example, this time relating the folk qualities of rock music to the declared 'authenticity' of the counter-culture, see Frith (1981).
3. There is a scene in the film *The Wanderers* (1979) that neatly captures this new social investment in pop. The leader of the

working-class Italo-American gang, the Wanderers (music: doo-wop, Dion, High School), following a girl down a street, stares through a window into the coffee house she has presumably entered and sees a young Bob Dylan performing 'The Times They Are A-Changin''. He turns away and goes back to his own community, leaving behind a striking image of culture and class.

9 SOUNDS OF YOUTH

If 'America' so clearly dominated images of leisure from the 1920s onwards, after the '40s the denounced 'foreignness' of popular culture was further amplified by the image of 'youth'.

Espresso Bongo © Raymond Rohauer (National Film Archive, London)

I had on precisely my full teenage drag . . . the grey pointed alligator casuals, the pink neon pair of ankle crepe nylon-stretch, my Cambridge blue glove-fit jeans, a vertical-striped happy shirt revealing my lucky neck-charm on its chain, and the Roman-cut short-arse jacket . . . not to mention my wrist identity jewel, and my Spartan warrior hair-do, which everyone thinks cost me 17/6d in Gerrard Street, Soho, but which I, as a matter of fact, do myself with a pair of nail-scissors and a three-sided mirror that Suzette's got, when I visit her flatlet up in Bayswater, W.2. (MacInnes, 1961, 23–4)

Youth, or better, the 'teenager', was apparently a post-1945 invention. It was also clearly American in origin. Before then teenagers simply did not exist, 'You were just an over-grown boy, or an under-grown man, life didn't seem to cater for anything whatever else between' (MacInnes, 1961, 27). This, of course, was not exactly true. Public youth styles existed before 1945. They stretch back through the razor gangs of the 1930s that inhabit Graham Greene's *Brighton Rock* into the nineteenth century, to the London 'coster-monger' and the northern 'scuttler' and his 'moll': 'bell-bottomed trousers, the heavy leather belt, pricked out in fancy designs with the large steel buckle and the thick, iron-shod clogs. His girl friend commonly wore clogs and shawl and a skirt with vertical stripes' (Roberts, 1973, 155). But the fact that the teenager was treated as something completely novel and alien to British culture was also true.

It was in the dislocating realities of the post-war world, in a landscape of recent rationing and recently filled-in bomb sites, that the image of money, clothes and music, rolled together into a distinctive youth style of coffee bars, clubs, dancing and American records, established the teenager as a provocative icon.

The appeal of a distinctive difference that could be put

together from available signs – musical styles and hair styles, reading habits and clothes, cinema images and personalized movement (the bike, the scooter, even how you walked) – was undoubtedly an attractive proposition when set against the daily predictability of your home, school, work and future. If you chose to subtract time from familiar circumstances, then suggestive sights and sounds could offer an alternative. Ron Barnes, a fledgling Teddy boy in the early 1950s: 'I dressed and acted as much as I could like my favourite gangster film star, Alan Ladd' (Barnes, 1976, 169).

The search for difference, for a youth 'identity', while encouraged by the imagery of consumerism, finds a deeper reason in the greater freedom of the imagination. It is here that we can begin to uncover some of the cultural co-ordinates that lay behind the teenage invasion of popular music in the 1950s.

'Don't knock the rock'

But before continuing with that story we need to pick up some of the threads we left trailing in America. For it was developments there in the late 1940s and early 1950s that were initially to provide many of the sounds that went into the subsequent remaking of British popular music under the impact of teenage tastes.

The importance of the copyright dispute between Tin Pan Alley and US radio stations in 1941 was that it had led to the stations setting up their own copyright organization which, forced to seek fresh material not controlled by the 'Alley', expanded the spectrum of radio music. What were previously considered marginal and regional styles – country and black music – received wider airing.

The break up of a centralized control over popular music and taste was then further accelerated with the introduction of recording tape at the end of the '40s. Recording tape, which was relatively cheap, yet robust and highly flexible – it could be cut, edited, and re-used – meant that small recording studios sprang up all over the country. There was no longer only an inaccessible record industry situated in New York or Los Angeles. Local

153

musics found an outlet on the spot. Fats Domino recorded in New Orleans; B. B. King, Rufus Thomas, Elvis and the early rock'n'rollers in Memphis; Roy Orbison and Buddy Holly in Clovis, New Mexico.

More accessible recording facilities and radio airplay promoted a mixture of the previously marginalized sounds of rhythm and blues and country music. The continual contact and crossing of these musics in the volatile culture of the South led to rockabilly, rock'n'roll: 'Aflash with images of sex, violence, and redneck existentialism' (Tosches, 1985, 8). Popularized in Britain by the records of Bill Haley, Elvis Presley, Chuck Berry, Jerry Lee Lewis and Little Richard, the music was adopted mainly by sections of working-class British youth as *their* sound around 1954–56. Like the exaggerated style of the already established Teddy boys, the musical excesses of rock'n'roll provided an exciting declaration with which you could reject your subordination and your position in the rigid prospects of British life.

It was Elvis Presley – R&B rhythms and country style, or, in Bill Haley's words, 'sex and sideburns' – who became on both sides of the Atlantic the symbol of rock'n'roll and teenage rebellion. Against this soundtrack, mean, moody and magnificent males – Elvis, James Dean, Marlon Brando, and anonymous Teddy boys – blown up in the dramatic hues of press photos, newsreels and films, momentarily appeared to threaten the comfortable stasis of the dull adult world of the 1950s. After hysterical press coverage of local cinema riots following the showing of Bill Haley's *Rock Around The Clock* (1956) it was a possibility difficult to ignore.

It was also, and remained, an image of a very male world of leather jackets, neon-lit nights, bikes, grease and cars; a tough street style that for women was only successfully, and briefly, occupied in the early 1960s by mainly black US girl groups: the Ronettes, Martha and the Vandellas, the Crystals, and the white Shangri-Las. But even these assertive voices sang from within subordination.

. . . the tough anonymous women in the female vocal groups did not sing about themselves but instead about their men who were 'Rebels' and 'Leader(s) of the Pack'. Their songs sang: 'He's So Fine', I wish he would 'Be My Baby', when he called me on the phone I pleaded 'Don't Hang Up', until 'One Fine Day' he walked me home, and 'Then He Kissed Me'. I knew that if I played my cards right I'd be 'Goin' to the Chapel' but of course, that was 'Easier Said than Done', 'Da Doo Ron Ron Ron, Da Doo Ron Ron'. (Chapple and Garofalo, 1977, 276)

While the images of America that had taken up residence in Swansea, Bradford and the Elephant and Castle were important, the music that accompanied it marked a turning point. In those days British popular music was a transatlantic mixture of crooners, native variety, and glamorous show business: Dickie Valentine, Alma Cogan, Rosemary Clooney, David Whitfield, Frankie Lane, Winifred Atwell, Shirley Bassey, Frank Sinatra, Nat 'King' Cole. After 1956 – the year of 'Heartbreak Hotel', 'Rock Around The Clock', 'Be Bop A Lula', 'Rip It Up' – ideas about popular music were shaken up as the field came to be divided between adult tastes and teenage 'pop'.

**Rhythm Crazed Teenagers Stampede in Manchester . . .
outside Gaiety Cinema after showing of _Rock Around the
Clock_ . . . Police powerless to deal with jiving youngsters
. . . Traffic was held up. . . .**

The British variant of US rock'n'roll and subsequent teenage pop music was weak and derivative. Slurred syllables and rushed rhythms were part of a particular musical encounter between black and white America. Separated from the experiences that had produced Elvis Presley, Wanda Jackson, Buddy Holly and the Everly Brothers, pop singers in Britain struggled to imitate the Stateside model. Cliff Richard tried hard with 'Move It' and Adam Faith looked suitably moody, but Tommy Steele ('Rock With the Caveman') betrayed his show-business predilections right from the beginning.

In Britain, in the 1950s and the early '60s, live appearances in theatres still remained important for pop music. So, a whole music hall, variety and theatrical tradition accompanied Britain's first stabs at rock'n'roll: Tommy Steele; the orange-haired, draped-jacketed, Wee Willie Harris. Later, Lonnie Donegan, with songs like 'My Old Man's a Dustman', would go directly back to music hall material.

Although the musical papers were extremely hesitant, British record companies – Decca, EMI, Philips, Pye – quickly stepped in to promote this native version of pop.[1] They were accompanied by slick entrepreneurs: John Kennedy, Tommy Steele's manager, anxious to give the music 'class'; and Larry Parnes who launched a succession of male singers with raunchy, mid-Atlantic, masculine names: Vince Eager, Marty Wilde, Billy Fury.

But while British show business, variety and television apparently absorbed the teenage threat, the revelatory sounds of rock'n'roll did not die without trace.[2] They had opened up an 'American connection' that had previously been restricted to the more secluded environs of jazz clubs and the Trad movement. And, if rock'n'roll was initially too exotic to be easily naturalized, a more accessible dip into America was found in skiffle.

Skiffle involved simple rhythms with lyrics drawn from black and white American folk music and the repertoires of singers like Huddie Ledbetter ('Leadbelly') and Woody Guthrie. In Britain it was originally heard in the Trad jazz revival in the early 1950s. Derived from the black 'spasm' bands of the 1920s and '30s, where a simple line-up of guitars, washboards, kazoos, and tea-chest basses provided the sounds, it was performed in both the Ken Coyler and Chris Barber bands. Lonnie Donegan, banjo player in the Barber band, went on to have a string of chart successes after 1956 with such skiffle numbers as 'Rock Island Line', 'Cumberland Gap', and 'Gambling Man'.

Skiffle became a popular craze in Britain in the years 1956–58. Its accessibility offered to a wide range of young people the possibility of approaching some of the excitement and novelty associated with rock'n'roll. An acoustic guitar, broom-stick bass, and improvised percussion, and you were away. It was the first American-derived music to be brought home and spread on a large scale, from inner-city jazz clubs out to bedrooms in suburbia. There were skiffle groups everywhere, in schools, housing estates and coffee bars; future members of the Shadows and the Beatles started out playing skiffle, as did Alexis Korner, the subsequent father of British urban blues. It provided an access to the interiors of American popular music, to a part of its hidden attraction; a route into the mysterious chemistry of rock'n'roll.[3]

Blues, beat and British

Another, slightly later route, which went even further into the territory of American popular music, was the select constituency of blues fans orbiting the jazz clubs in the late '50s and early '60s. Alexis Korner's Blues Incorporated was the first group to gain notice here, but it was the Rolling Stones and their white R&B successors (the Pretty Things, the Yardbirds, the Animals, the Kinks, Manfred Mann, Them), that went on to collaborate with the Merseyside synthesis of the Beatles in realizing a distinctly 'English' pop sound in the early 1960s.

In London and crowded provincial clubs in Liverpool, Manchester, Birmingham and Newcastle, young men, often art-school drop-outs, drew directly on black American music and memories of the excitement of rock'n'roll to produce a loud dancing music and distinctive sound. Once it had achieved some initial success, first with the Beatles and then the Rolling Stones, the source of much of this excitement, often as distant from white America as it was from Britain, became public. Whether it was the studio sound of the black girl groups (the Ronettes, Martha and the Vandellas, the Shirelles, the Supremes), the older, rougher Chicago club sound of Muddy Waters, John Lee Hooker and Howlin' Wolf, or the new black synthesis of soul music (James Brown, Otis Redding, Mary Wells, Marvin Gaye), Afro-American music began to occupy the charts and, thanks to *Ready, Steady, Go!*, British television screens.

Ready, Steady, Go! began broadcasting every Friday evening in August 1963. It was a 'mod' programme. Its connection, however tenuous, to the 'hip' codes of the mod subculture set the pace. Smartly dressed youth danced, against a Pop Art decor, to the music of visiting American blues and soul singers, as well as to the Beatles, the Stones, Dusty Springfield, the Who, Sandie Shaw, the Animals, Lulu, the Kinks. In its combination of youth and style, of music and fashion, it was *the* programme of the moment: pop music, pop culture, 'swinging London'.

With television exposure and the world-wide success of its music, British youth culture went public. The Carnaby Street mod became Saturday-afternoon youth in any of Britain's major cities. Pop culture and images of youth began to enter areas from which they had previously been excluded: the 'quality' press and Sunday colour supplements; later, 'high brow' late-night viewing on BBC 2. More obvious class and cultural lines, such as those that had excluded the Teds and rock'n'roll music in the 1950s, were blurred in an expanding taste for the catchy songs of the Beatles and the more fashionable icons of the moment: mini-skirts, Biba, Mary Quant, Twiggy.

Britain today is a society stifling for lack of any art that expresses the experience of living in it. Our theatre is a quaint anachronism, our novel is dead, and our cinema a mere obituary of it. Perhaps the only art form which has an authentic expressive vitality in England is pop music. It at least reflects back to us the immediate constituents of experience, even when it does not illuminate them. It is no accident that it is the one product of contemporary British

culture which has any international currency. (Merton, 1968, 31)

The unprecedented success of the Beatles and of British pop widened the music's potential constituency. Pop supplemented and sometimes completely replaced jazz and classical music in many students' digs and middle-class homes. After the mid-1960s, it acquired an increasing cosmopolitan tone and public autonomy; its signs were now collected into a more global frame, into a counter-proposal, into a counter-culture.

Counter-culture

Members of the counter-culture, unlike the mods or the Teds, did not propose to work over the surfaces of consumerism and daily urban life, but to withdraw from them. The psychedelic music of Jimi Hendrix, Jefferson Airplane and Pink Floyd connotated the sensual, strobe-lit, drugged interiors of a 'trip' to an 'elsewhere' that the 'straight' establishment had no hope of entering or comprehending. Inside this reality, the music, increasingly less structured, was prone to improvisation, 'jams', and displays of individual prowess. Music was itself considered a force for change, it could 'turn you on' to a new order of things. 'When the mode of the music changes, the walls of the city SHAKE!', declared the cover of the ninth issue of *The International Times* (later *IT*).

This 'alternative reality', laconically fixed in the distinctive style of the hippy, came to fruition in the mythological land of perpetual sun and endless surf where the wave of youth never breaks: California. California, where Hollywood researches the icons of tomorrow and dreams drive the everyday soul. California, where fantasy turns to fact in a symbiotic pleasure dome of nature and culture: fibreglass surf boards and the sea, concrete freeways and deserts, sprawling steel-glass cities and the open promise of space.

Like the surfer, the dragster, the custom car freak, and the hot rod racer, the hippy was also intent on exploring a particular version of the 'Californian Dream'; that physical and metaphorical promise of the West. Under the Californian sun, astrology, mysticism, millenarianism and sometimes madness, were often not far from this privileged communion with the promise. Hippies – men and women in long hair (Adam and Eve: nature's couple); sandals, jeans and maternity dresses; smoking 'grass'; 'tripping' on LSD or else 'high' on natural 'vibes'; their bodies swaying in the Garden to the warm waves of rock music – attempted to exit from the abundance of white, middle America and occupy a fragile dream.

What made the hippies stand out and turned them into an international symbol was ultimately their ability to function as a complex sign for the youth rebellion that swept the States and Europe in the late 1960s. By then an 'underground' of musical and literary origins met up with the unrest on university campuses on both sides of the Atlantic and acquired a decisive political shape. The subsequent protest against authoritarian structures in all walks of life, and against the massive war the United States was waging in Vietnam, sparked off a series of

161

incidents that culminated in May 1968 when it spilled over into the streets of Paris.

That the roots of that revolt were deeply compromised – the 'oppressed' were invariably white, male, highly educated and middle class – does not eradicate the contradictions it exposed: the promise of the present and its failure to deliver.

In Britain, all this tended to occur on a different scale. Emotional and symbolic investment rarely touched either the point of later Californian psychosis or the Parisian spring. The green mound of Somerset's Glastonbury Tor, for astrological and mythological reasons a favoured hippy site, has little in common with the dramatic nature of southern California where various communes (including Charles Manson's Family) camped out on the edge of the desert and strange scenarios were rehearsed. And if politics in the British counter-culture were disruptive they rarely managed the heady idealism of the Parisian *enragés*. They leaned more towards the liberation of a specific 'situation'. Some were immediately important, the discovery of secret files and the undemocratic structure of university decision making, for example. Others owed more to Groucho than to Karl Marx: repainting the Vice-Chancellor's house without consulting him on the colour scheme, or staging a nude-in.

But 1968 passed, and the romantic belief that the music might 'break on through to the other side' (the Doors), although temporarily sustained by the Woodstock festival the following year, was cruelly mocked in the violent breakdown of the Rolling Stones' free concert at Altamont in California only three months later.[4] Playing with freedom – 'Do your own thing', 'Let it all hang out' – on the symbolic edge of the civilized world, the West Coast, Jagger, the Stones, and the counter-culture discovered that you could get badly burnt, even destroyed by the strange tribes released from the Californian Id. Fantasy turned into ugly facts: Hell's Angels terrorized the Altamont crowd and murdered the 18-year-old black youth Meredith Hunter; Charles Manson's Family left a trail of corpses across southern California, amongst them the body of film actress Sharon Tate. It was time to retreat.

Rock – already a social step up the ladder from 'pop' – now became the haven of 'musicians' and 'artists'; its link to the promise of the counter-culture dropped away, leaving behind the drugs, a vague idealism, and a 'freedom' to make a lot of money and translate yesterday's slogans into good advertising copy: 'The Man Can't Bust Our Music' (CBS Records). But the 'hype' was not the record companies'. They made no mystery about their aims. It was rock music itself that confused the issues. It took the counter-cultural 'alternative' and slowly transformed it into the separate world of art. Once there it chose to ignore the irony of the evidence – LPs, the preferred channel of 'progressive rock' music, were now out-selling 45s – and claimed that rock was non-commercial.[5]

From its sweaty days in the R&B clubs, dance halls and one-niters in the early 1960s, British pop music had gone through a lot of changes. It had found Stateside success, been absorbed by the counter-culture and picked up a new higher education audience, forgotten much of its debt to black music, and emerged by 1970 inside an international rock format. Intent on proving its new 'artistic' credentials, it doodled in lengthy and often boring improvisations, adopted classical music forms and produced a series of mutants of varying success: folk-rock, jazz-rock, country-rock, orchestrated-rock.[6]

On the radio

In Britain, rock music was not the only music available. Although looking at *Melody Maker*, *New Musical Express* and the newly established *Sounds* in the early 1970s you couldn't be blamed for thinking so. If you turned on the radio you would hear something very different. Radio music had been reorganized and updated after the success of the pirate stations in the British beat boom. And since the early 1970s, the four BBC channels (of which Radio One is for pop) have been joined by some eighty independent local radio stations. While, by the end of the decade, a few specialized programmes for reggae and soul music were occasionally cropping up in the evening, for daytime listening there was, and remains, mainstream pop and male DJ chatter ostensibly directed at a housewife public ('ridiculous in these days of high unemployment', Sheryl Garratt).

The music, once the soundtrack to the 'chance to transgress' in the 'excessive social exchanges' of dancing and parties (Coward, 1984), is offered as a retro-soundscape for the domestication of desire. To stir the memory and induce reverie in the midst of household work it relies on a mixture of 'golden oldies' and contemporary 'middle of the road' sounds. But whether the listeners' pleasure directly corresponds to that 'message', whether women are prisoners of the radio, unable to invest other desires in the voice of Tom Jones, Abba, Kate Bush or Rod Stewart, seems doubtful.

Radio music is where, more than anywhere else, pop has its daily currency. And as a cultural medium compounded of social, sexual, racial and emotional tissues, popular radio music presents a continual recycling of the expected, the assumed, the inoffensively safe. Such predictability is an ambiguous quality, however. It creates distance, irony, knowledge. The pleasure in listening to such programmes, to phoning in, and generally participating, is not necessarily naive: it can arise from the recognition of distance, from a pleasure in its transitory abolition, rather than an absorption in an obsessive identification. While the radio can become the echo chamber of your desires, its limits are not necessarily your own.

Moving on up: black music and into the '80s

Meanwhile, the popularity of soul music in the mid-1960s, although driven underground once the local mod crusade had been replaced by the international references of the counter-culture, had not been extinguished. The taste for the exotic in black music found a continuation (and shared subcultural lineage) in the skinheads and Jamaican ska music of the late 1960s, around the time the 'alternative society' was celebrating its own arrival in Hyde Park, and in the energetic dancing and stylized attention to obsure US soul music in the clubs and dance halls of the 'Northern Soul' circuit which also sprang up in those years.[7]

But the music that most clearly developed underground, in the black and gay cultures of New York City in the early 1970s, was disco.

The 'sound' . . . is the sound of a 20,000 dollar DJ system with three turntables, immense coffin-shaped speakers and tweeters hung separate from the woofers enabling discs with a lot of highs to propel the human body into perpetual motion. You'll find such sound systems in night clubs who've ditched live music for the disco action, in warehouses converted into party palaces with a system and some strobes. You'll find the amplified blare of the sweet beat booming across America and Europe but you'll find it at its most hectic and frenetic in the whirling crystal ball world of New York City. (Cummings, 1975, 8)

DJs, such as the famous Francis at The Sanctuary in New York, laid track over track to set up an uninterrupted dancing pattern that kept bodies in motion all night long. The music, engineered for the ostentatious styles of the dance floor, was despised by rock musicians: 'Disco sucks'. It was considered to represent the triumph of commerce over musical taste. But then the same verdict was applied to most black music at the time. Disco, meanwhile, as dance, as body music, revealed a further history.

Out on the floor, in particular clubs and venues, it suggested an important alternative as Afro-American and Hispanic rhythms enveloped the body in rhythms and diffused the phallocentric beat of white rock music (Dyer, 1979b). It became the central sound (although by no means only here) in the formation of gay culture in the 1970s, and was carried over into the 1980s in the music and explicit sentiments of such groups as Frankie Goes To Hollywood and Bronski Beat.

But the effects of disco stretch even further across the economy of pop. The later electronic syntax of rap and 'scratch' mixing and 'the pastiche possibilities of multi-track recording' (Bergman, 1985), the experimental collages in white pop after punk, the commitment to dance and rhythmic disciplines in music in the '80s, all owe much to the sounds developed in disco.

But these later connections were relatively public compared to the presence of another sound, that of Jamaican reggae. This music was identified not with a subculture but with a community. Already in the 1950s, West Indian music was present in Britain, particularly in London around Soho in clubs like the Flamingo, the Sunset, the 77 Club. There you could hear the lewd calypso lyrics of Lord Kitchener and the Mighty Sparrow and the early sounds of ska before it changed into rocksteady and then reggae. But by the 1970s, Trojan Records and small independent labels like Klik, Tropical and Grove Music were supplying reggae to black Britons rather than to older immigrants reliving memories of the West Indies.

The deep, strangely tripping bass, the almost indecipherable patois of the lyrics and the jerky off-beat scratchiness of the trebly guitar rhythms, betrayed the roots. Reggae, like salsa and other Hispanic rhythms and textures, was another 'hot sauce' to be brought by immigrants out of the Caribbean and Latin America into metropolitan pop music in the 1970s (Bergman, 1985).

In the beginning, except for the skinheads, who on the lookout for a language of group identity had transferred their allegiance from North America to Kingston, Jamaica, and its local 'rude boy' style, nobody outside the black community was interested. And even the skins had to call a halt when reggae shifted from 'rude' concerns and street machismo to Rasta-farianism: the apocalyptic tones of black redemption and a return to Africa preached by dreadlocked Rastas offered no haven for white exiles.

What drove the music and black identity together down the channel of Rastafarianism was the brutal reality of racism. Unwilling quietly to accept their lot in the hostile cities of white Britain, black youth discovered the possibility of translating their daily experience of racism, urban poverty and a forced marginality into the religious 'sufferin'' of the Rasta. Through reggae music and the success of the late Bob Marley, young

166

blacks learnt that Britain is part of 'Babylon' and that Africa (in particular, Ethiopia) is the 'Promised Land'.

The 'concrete jungles' of Bob Marley's 'JA' were transferred to the 'Front Line' in Brixton; St Paul's, Bristol; Handsworth, Birmingham. The style of Rasta – dreadlocks, wearing the Ethiopian colours of red, green and gold, speaking in a patois thick with metaphor – became common. It provided the language, symbology and ubiquitous sounds for a self-referring black identity ('I is I') that had no need of the white world.

Although a few reggae performers found widespread success – Bob Marley, Peter Tosh, Black Uhuru – it has been the sustenance of reggae's 'black truth' that has maintained its power and presence in Britain. Now it may be hip to acknowledge its sounds, and since punk and politics in the late '70s it has become a 'legitimate' music for some whites (including the record companies). But it is in the specialist reggae shops, under the more than 100 independent reggae labels operating in Britain, at all-night 'sheebens' and 'blues' parties, and not through radio airplay (except for such pirate stations as London's Dread Broadcasting Corporation) or the absent chart exposure its sales often justify, that the music survives and grows.

The dense syntax of reggae, like the twisted rhythms of bebop, the testifying groans, shouts and shrieks of the blues, gospel and soul music, and the exclamatory sidewalk anthems of rap, push the previously repressed, hidden and inarticulate into sound. In the interchange between black oral cultures and electricity, between the distilled languages of experience and recording technology, the music and the human voice frequently cross 'a space somewhere between speech and scream' (Toop, 1984, 53).

In jazz and Jamaican 'dub', in the 'talking' guitar of Jimi Hendrix, and more recently in New York's 'scratch' and rap music, the voice is transferred to instrumental and electronic timbres, and there pushed in directions and spaces previously only explored by the avant-garde. Bop musicians 'scrambling' well known tunes of the day and Grandmaster Flash simultaneously 'cutting up' soul, disco and rock records to create a

'**There are no words because it is a language in itself.**' (Disc Jockey Lee Garrett in Haralambos, 1974, 54)

furious collage 'displacing familiarity' (Toop, 1984, 18), are both pursuing a black music tradition of dislocating the popular to show 'where it's at'.

Instruments – drums, saxophones, guitars, studio mixers, microphones, turntables ('wheels of steel') – become extensions of your self, technology is socialized and bent to particular cultural rhythms. Twelve-inch records – grooves with room to move, cut-up and 'scratch' – are filled with words from the street, and rap, the latest in the black urban soundtrack, hits the international record racks.

Being black, being poor, being cool, Hollywood, street gangs, Hong Kong Kung Fu movies, James Brown's funk, Atari video games, block parties, mammoth decorated Japanese cassette players ('boxes', 'ghetto blasters'), sports wear, computerized rhythms, dark glasses, disco music, dreadlocks, salsa, mixing boards, cut-up sounds, graffiti, break dancing – it all stewed in the cultural cauldron of the Bronx and in the late '70s

released the black male street style of 'hip hop culture' to the rest of the world.[8]

New York's music finds a home in London and suggests to black (and white) 'crews' in Britain a new identity as they break dance amongst the Saturday-morning shoppers in Covent Garden. Another style, another language, another opportunity to present your 'self' in the contemporary metropolis.

Out of chaos

When in 1966 the Rolling Stones, by then the favourite targets of moral outrage, presented themselves in drag to promote the single 'Have You Seen Your Mother, Baby, Standing in the Shadow?', a glittering, androgynous future was staked out for male pop music. This mixing of sounds, sexual codes and deliberate shock, further distilled through the dark aesthetics of the New York group and Andy Warhol associates, The Velvet Underground, eventually became the *leit-motif* for the musical mannerisms of David Bowie. Bowie's transitory egos – whether they came from Mars or Weimar Germany – were the dandified heroes of a camp subversion. Through his testing of tastes and playing with the stylized signs of sex, Bowie rapidly ran through a repertoire that the rest of the decade spent exploring.

Relating sex to subversion and signs to shock was, of course, the twilight zone privileged by punk, ergo the nomenclature: The Sex Pistols, The Clash, The Damned, Johnny Rotten, Sid Vicious. In 1976, against a background in which the stylistic connections between music, youth and fashion had long been established and accepted, punk managed to produce a self-conscious style of crisis. The 'dumbest' face of subcultures proved to be the vehicle of some rather intellectual activity. Revivalist Teddy boys physically assaulted punks for 'being too clever'.

With punk, the traditional closure of subcultural style was subverted as it became the object of facetious quotations, irreverent cut-ups and ironic poses. Punks ransacked post-war subcultures for fashions and signs to re-cycle and re-live. In a blasphemous remixing of revered subcultural memories the

170

London's
Living Guide

Time Ou

A new generation of rockers
gathers at the Lyceum.

Born Too Late?

The second time round the faithful reproduction of subcultural style
refers back to the now solid referents of the past, a history safe for
nostalgia and cultural conservatism:
the very concept of 'revival' in the 1970s gave the teddy
boys an air of legitimacy. After all, in a society which
seemed to generate a bewildering number of fads and
fashions, the teddy boys were a virtual institution: an
authentic, albeit dubious part of the British heritage.
(Hebdige, 1979, 82)

171

sartorial signs of Teddy boy, mod and skinhead simultaneously hung in patchwork array from the same skinny shoulders, the same physical clothes-hanger, the same sign carrier. The punks constructed an iconography of disrespect, pillaging the sub-cultural past and attiring themselves in urban rubbish: bin-liner skirts, empty sweet packets pinned on ripped and torn clothing. Here we discover 'statement dressing', a 'shocking' punctuation of the public narratives of the everyday. Clothes as 'our weapons, our challenges, our visible insults' (Carter, 1982); a sartorial parody of the social and economic crisis of the late '70s.

Punk emerged as an angry noise in the centre of white pop music. It began in London clubs, quickly spread to the provinces, and soon afterwards reappeared inside the record industry. The music was short, sharp and loud: lyrics shouted in an exaggerated naive style supported (or, more frequently, overwhelmed) by a barrage of frantic guitars and brutal drumming. It was a rude blast directed against the pretentious dominion of rock music.

It was do-it-yourself pop, music from below, your own sound, 'white roots'.

But the 'roots' in this case were ambiguous. For some they represented a mythical 'authenticity', the base line for political and group identities. This is The Clash, Rock Against Racism, and punk as 'white reggae' (Johnny Rotten).[9] Later, this would also lead to the hard punk exit of skinhead fundamentalism and a refusal to betray the 'street sounds' of '76. For others, the 'roots', the icons of authenticity, represented ironic quotations of a lost innocence. Inside the circuits of contemporary representation – the press, television, the record industry – they were signs that served to disrupt the status quo; signs designed to provoke.

Punk marked a turning point in British youth styles. The self-conscious constructions – the deliberate choice of imagery guaranteed to shock: the swastika, the mutilation of the body by safety pins, its imprisonment in chains and dog collars – turned the attention of subsequent youth culture to the actual mechanisms of representation: the codes themselves.

This has turned out to be as true for music as for clothes. The musical chaos that punk proposed forced a stark reappraisal of

The Sex Pistols apotheosized rock and roll, as if the music were a tape played backwards, erasing itself as it played. (Michael Freedberg)

pop's own sounds. The simple distinction between 'mainstream' and margin, between avant-garde and popular, between music and 'noise' were confused. The singular history of pop, seen as a set of successive waves – rock'n'roll, beat, progressive rock – was set aside and replaced by multiple histories. Crossover and synthesize becomes the choice: black rhythms and heavy metal, funk and punk, jazz and beat.

The resulting collage produces a frame in which diverse musical styles co-exist and combine – rockabilly and '60s soul, acoustic music and programmed drum machines, 'roots' reggae

173

and computerized keyboards; where different rhythms are drawn from the global drum; where voices are retrieved from the past and remixed for the present (i.e. Keith LeBlanc and Malcolm X's 'No Sell Out').[10] The mainstream – the records that are chosen for publicity and promotion, that make money – remains, but, and now in the 1980s, it is flanked on several sides by an increasingly cosmopolitan repertoire in which the sounds of Africa and America, of New York and London, of the old and the new, not only co-exist, but quote and recall one another.

Between the grooves

By way of a conclusion, I simply want to redirect attention to the structure of the argument in the previous chapters. In chapter 7, we saw that popular music in Britain, centred on London and the music hall, was already well on its way to becoming a commercially organized industry by the 1880s. The record, destined to accelerate this process and to eventually offer new possibilities to previously unknown musics, had already appeared. Here we noticed, despite the strong disapproval of many authorities, a growing taste for American music and dance styles, favoured in particular by the rise of the cinema.

At this point, with the popularity of ragtime and jazz, the hidden dimension of black, Afro-American music began to appear. For the moment (1900–40), it tended to be translated by white performers into sounds and dances acceptable to Tin Pan Alley and Hollywood. But the growth of the radio, and cheaper recording facilities, finally permitted hidden American musics – in particular country music and rhythm and blues – to challenge Tin Pan Alley's hold on popular taste.

Through the popularity of dance, records, radio and cinema, popular music provided spaces for social, sexual and stylized encounters. From the 1920s onwards a mixture of youth, dance, and increasingly American-derived musics dominated many a Saturday night. It was a tendency that was decisively deepened in the 1950s after the public identification of the 'teenager' with a distinctive 'pop' music.

(David Johnson)

In these chapters we have followed a story that involves a battle over musical and cultural taste. A story where, in clubs and dance halls, in the record industry and musical press, on radio and television – that is, inside the commercial structures of popular culture – social, sexual, racial and generational identities and discriminations have been fought over and contested.

I have concentrated on the more obvious elements: on the centrality of commercial enterprise, recording technology, black music and youth. It is a story, at least in its more public face, that betrays gaps and silences. For example, of how pop music has been predominantly occupied with male street sounds (from Elvis through beat music to Bruce Springsteen and break

An exception: Sade plays Deptford. (David Johnson)

Only punk created sufficient confusion to widen the spaces temporarily. But since then male gender-bending (Boy George, Marilyn) and gay, 'boystown' music continue to hold public attention as the boys construct and control their images. However, apart from such independent figures as Patti Smith, Tina Turner and Chrissie Hynde, the large female following for Madonna, and the adverse criticism she regularly receives in the male-dominated musical press, suggests a new self-management in public female iconography, with women exiting from bedroom culture and male criticism into that of the streets.

dancing) and has consistently marginalized women: the 'ghosts in the hit machine' who are usually relegated to 'back-up' vocals and almost totally excluded from record production, instrumental work and DJ-ing (Steward and Garratt, 1984).[11]

To conclude, however, on a note of change. Inside the hard centre of the '80s, sounds and sentiments – which may be the heavy rap of Run DMC, the bitter-sweet sound and explicit politics of The Style Council or the influential female 'street' iconography of Madonna – continue to overflow into the imprecise networks of the everyday with a potential to invest our lives with the fantasy, romance, hope and movement of its pulse; with its promise of always 'something more'.

Notes

1. With the success of rock'n'roll and subsequent teenage pop music, US record labels began in the 1950s to abandon their licensing agreements with EMI and Decca and set up their own output labels in Britain. A decade later, and with the triumph of rock music, American labels like CBS and Warner Brothers commanded a major slice of the British market. For further details on the organization of the British recording industry, see Frith (1978).

2. For an excellent review of what in fact turned out to be an extremely troubled marriage between British television and pop music, see Tasker (1982).

3. In the mystique of words and argot located in the geography of the imagination, the names of US cities and highways – New York, Chicago, Route 66, LA – have found a resonance in Britain that British equivalents have never managed to challenge.

4. The Maysles brothers' film *Gimme Shelter*, shot in sombre black and white, and with Jagger crying in front of the moviola as Meredith Hunter is stabbed and beaten to death by the Angels, starkly captures the counter-culture nightmare of Altamont.

5. Of course, this self-deception goes on all the time in the traditional circles of artistic production. It is the immediate

proximity to the blatant commercial processes of popular culture, where the rhetoric of 'taste' is bluntly translated into the explicit strategies of distribution and markets, and 'value' into transitory sales figures, that makes it much more difficult to sustain. In the 1960s, Pop Art wisely celebrated the irony; in the early 1970s, rock music tried to disguise it in a worldly cynicism.

6. Before disco gained wide popularity and punk finally tore up its pretensions, rock music was challenged by the emergence from within its own ranks of 'heavy metal'. This loud, guitar-centred music – Led Zeppelin, Deep Purple, Black Sabbath, etc. – attracted an audience composed of long-haired, working-class males and students. Its popularity and rocker-macho imagery continues right down to the present, and, along with 'Northern Soul', must rank as one of Britain's longest-standing musical cultures.

7. The importance of soul music in British youth cultures for establishing radical differences and drawing the line between 'them' and 'us', should not obscure its diverse, more complex, centrality in black populism. Take James Brown: he sings 'Sex Machine' but he also 'reveals a belief and faith in conventional morality and the protestant ethic as a means to happiness and fulfillment' (Haralambos, 1974, 117). '(Say It Loud) I'm Black And I'm Proud' goes alongside 'Don't Be A Dropout'.

8. The thin plot of the film *Beat Street* (1984) probably helps rather than hinders its presentation of the Bronx and hip-hop culture. You get to see Grandmaster Flash, The Treacherous Three, Afrika Bambaataa and the Zulu Nation, and lots of break dancing. There is also the video *Hip-Hop, A Street History* (PGV).

9. Punk's 'white riot', even if it only existed in the disruptive order of subcultural collage, saw in reggae music and the apocalyptic language of Rastafarianism a further confirmation of its own refusal. In Britain, white rebellion and black redemption discovered a transitory affinity: Bob Marley recorded 'Punky Reggae Party' and in July 1977, on Capital Radio, Johnny Rotten talked of his interest in reggae and the music of Dr Alimantado, Fred Locks and Aswad. It was on this punk-reggae

alliance that the successful Rock Against Racism campaign was largely built.

10. This collage is largely sustained by electronics – whether it's hearing a rhythm on the radio, finding a particular sound on an old record or micro-computer technology. In the last case the very language of music undergoes transformation. For, besides the spectacle of video, there is the new exchange of sound and image that occurs directly through the keyboard of the contemporary synthesizer. With digital computer technology sounds are turned into images that can be stretched, modulated and compressed, the music is transformed into 'sound paintings' – a 'graphics pallete, "coating" sounds as if with an airbrush' (Lipman, 1985). Here playing music approaches the contemporary discipline of design.

11. See Steward and Garratt (1984) and Chapple and Garofalo (1977).

Suggestions for further work

1. What sort of evidence suggests that urban popular music in Britain was already a thoroughly commercial institution by the 1880s?

2. Indicate some of the many roads that black music – from ragtime to reggae and rap – has had to travel in the world of popular music, and what, in various moments, it might culturally be said to represent.

3. The means of electronic transmission – records, radio and recording technology – have destroyed certain cultural distances, permitting access to new experiences, new possibilities. For example, the popularity of US blues and R&B in Britain in the late 1950s and early 1960s, or the influence of recording technology on reggae particularly in the case of 'dub'. See if you can illustrate this tendency with further examples and details.

4. One of the histories that exists inside pop music is that which connects sounds to sexuality, most obvious in the evident centrality of dance. Yet, while certain images have been highly visible (i.e. those concerned with male heterosexuality), others have often remained invisible. Try and give some examples that

illustrate the shift in the form these relations have taken over the years, for women and men.

5. Despite the industrial organization and corporation imagery of the record industry it is frequently incapable of foreseeing what will happen to the music it distributes once it hits the dance floor, the air waves and the record shops. This suggests that a neat distinction between the 'good' and the 'bad' side of popular music, between a marginal, and presumably 'alternative', music and more mainstream fare is not always as useful as it might seem. Both are equally dependent upon commercial structures for their production and distribution – from the recording studio to the musical press. Drawing on your own experience and tastes try and indicate how the pleasure and sense of music might cut across the simple distinction between incorporated and oppositional pop music.

PART FOUR
CONCLUSIONS

10 IN THESE TIMES

Contemporary popular culture, as we noted at the beginning of this book, is an urban phenomenon. Living in the city we inherit its physical structures and cultural conditions. In challenging *and* exploring this inheritance much of our urban 'sense' and 'self' is formed. For the metropolis is a psychological as well as a physical reality, a cultural as well as economic environment.

The city exists as a series of doubles: it has official and hidden cultures, it is a real place and a site of the imagination. Its elaborate network of streets, housing, public buildings, transport systems, parks and shops is paralleled by a complex of attitudes, habits, customs, expectancies, and hopes that reside in us as urban subjects. We discover that urban 'reality' is not singular but multiple, that inside the city there is always another city.

The city is also a dirty sign, contaminated by different cultures, different forces, different desires, different needs that accumulate in the metropolitan body. And there is no guarantee that they are commensurable: there exists 'a surplus of meaning' (Laclau, 1986).

Despite the intentions of architects and city planners to reduce the city to an abstract, rational order and geometrical purity, to a 'skeletal structure' (Mies van der Rohe), it remains a body redolent with the diverse richness and eroticism of the 'here and now'.

And marks on the skin, on the surface of the metropolitan

body, can turn out to be as important as the underlying source or 'unity' we might assign to them. For it is on the surfaces that history intersects with desire; it is there that identities are realized. This is the place of sense.

David Hockney, **A Bigger Splash** (Tate Gallery, London)

The montage of the present

Life is a cut-up. (William Burroughs)

It's the way you actually use it, and not the actual record itself that's important. (Max of Mastermind sound system)

I would say that montage is concerned with bits as bits,

not as fragments broken from some original whole . . . /and/ the politics of montage concerns the way in which we take up with practices (literature, science . . . sex) as assemblages, indeed as montages, and not as monolithic wholes. (Yves Lomax; Stephen Heath; Gilles Deleuze and Felix Guattari; Lisa Tickner; in Tickner (1984))

The sights and sounds of the urban scene – advertising, music, cinema, television, fashion, magazines, video clips – exist in the rapid circuits of electronic production/reproduction/distribution. They are not unique artefacts but objects and events multiplied a thousand, a million times over. In the rapid interplay of these signs, sense outstrips the referents. It produces an aesthetics of transitory and tactile reception, of immediate participation and expendable criteria. Contemplation and study can follow (i.e. film studies, books on pop music, television, popular culture, etc.), but, in a medium in which we have all become 'experts', *it is not a necessary requirement.*

In this collage of sights and sounds we discover the immediate co-ordinates of the present: where existing meanings and views, ideas and opinions, are reproduced; where social practices are formed and experienced; where both consensus and rebellion is voiced; where dogma and innovation, prejudice and change, find expression.

Contemporary urban culture, then, is a complex cypher of its circumstances. Across its multiple surfaces a popular semiotics daily mixes together real conditions and imaginary material. The vivid languages of the cinema, television, pop music and magazines are translated into personalized styles, manners, tastes and pleasures: under given conditions, in particular situations, we take reality to pieces in order to put it back together with a further gain in meaning. The signs are inhabited, appropriated, domesticated.

The signs are inhabited. Cinema suggests the architecture of the city, and the city the scenarios of the cinema: the skylines of apocalypse, overloaded with images of imminent collapse, from Fritz Lang's *Metropolis* (1926) to Ridley Scott's *Blade Runner* and Terry Gilliam's *Brazil* (1984). Meanwhile, in the everyday world, the ambients of Dan Dare and Flash Gordon become part of architectural syntax and demonstrate the power of the image over 'reality'; what Jean Baudrillard calls the power of the languages of simulation, or hyper-reality, to replace the 'real'. Signs become seemingly more pertinent than what they supposedly refer to, Disneyland more 'real' than Los Angeles (Baudrillard, 1983a).

The signs are inhabited. Since punk started 'playing with reality', and, cutting up its subcultural past for stylistic options, spectacularly demonstrated the continual mutability of the same signs, youth style has become institutionalized as a contemporary art: collage dressing for the '80s – Steve Strange and the Blitz kids, 'Cabaret Futura', the success of magazines like *The Face* and *i-D*, the clothes galleries of Hyper Hyper and Kensington Market – exhibiting and 'quoting' styles in a continual sartorial research on the contemporary 'I'.

Clothes, sounds and styles transform the day-time of school, work and unemployment into an extended night-time where, if nothing else, you control your own time, your own body, your own fantasies: 'compensation for the loss in a universal reality is sought in the security of the code' (Brooks, 1984).

186

vibes

'His almonds need darning ... you stupid alphonse.'

'There are languages other than words, languages of symbol and languages of nature. There are languages of the body. And prizefighting is one of them. Boxing is a rapid debate between two sets of intelligence. It takes place rapidly because it is conducted with the body rather than the mind. If this seems extreme, let us look for a connection.
Picasso could never do arithmetic when he was young because the number seven looked to him like a nose turned upside down. So to learn arithmetic would slow him up. He was a future painter - his intelligence resided somewhere in the coordination of the body and the mind. He was not going to cut off his body from his mind by learning numbers. But most of us do. We have minds which work fairly well and bodies which sometimes don't. But if we are white and went to be comfortable we put our emphasis on learning to talk with the mind. Ghetto cultures, black, Puerto Rican and Chicano cultures having less expectation of comfort tend to stick with the wit their bodies provide. They speak to each other with their bodies, they signal with their clothes. They talk with many a silent telepathic intelligence. And doubtless feel the frustration of being unable to express the subtleties of their state in words, just as the average middle-class white will feel unable to carry out his dreams of glory by the uses of his body.'
Extract from Black Fists, by Norman Mailer.

THE LANGUAGE OF FASHION

The language of fashion is not restricted to mere garments. It's a language of signs and symbols, noise and movements, light and form and colours that describe the world we perceive and express our perceptions. The units of the language are beaten out on the pavements of London then sent hurtling across the ocean to New York to be broken down by Black America. The sense is mashed up, re-arranged and sent back to us on Sugarhell or Tommy Boy or somesuch

The lights and movements and colours of this language crushed into a quantel paintbox and pureed through a cathode-ray tube are displayed on Fridays between five and seven o'clock. We look and listen, pay close attention, then mispronounce and make spelling mistakes until we are satisfied with our new sentences.

Eloquence and wit, clarity and conviction are essentials for public address. Jazz dancers and breakers and good old-fashioned Soulboys/girls speak of sheer and sexual elation, they twitch and step, flutter, kick and spin.

Fig.5: ALTERNATIVE DISGUISE
WINSTON DETLEIV, singer and acoustic guitarist with SEVENTH SEANCE. Their fourth single 'The Anguish Of Love' is out soon; it features ex-Marc and The Maabas cellist Martin McGarrick, and is totally acoustic. They will also have a Janice Long session and an album coming in the near future. Jacket: Poplar Market, £10; Gloves & Trousers Oxfam; Jewellery Top Shop; Diamante earring Oxford St; Bracelet Poplar Market; Brooch from antiques fair; Guitar: Eros, Hornsey junk shop, £20.

There's still a lot to be said for the wink.
M. Jagger

Check out 'A Whole Lot Of Ways (To Catch A Fish)' by SPY, out now on Mission Discs

WORD PLAY

The Great British Style is one of free speech. This is due mainly to the conceptual orientation of the English language, with its emphasis on richness and depth and abhorrence of repetition. Metaphor is highly valued, a variety of verbs exist for most actions (e.g.) Walk = stroll, plod, saunter, amble, trudge, slope, shuffle, lurch, waddle, and so on ...) and there are delicate nuances that differentiate synonyms.

All these qualities find parallels in our sartorial expression. Just as we detach words from their literal meanings and use them figuratively, as in a 'sharp' tongue, 'foot' of the mountain, or a family 'tree' so swimwear becomes evening dress. T-shirts become lords, neckties reach kneecaps and heads get bashed through. 180. As long as people continue to invent new words and phrases, or redefine old or existing articles, the language of clothes is a living thing.

The creamy whirring sound of a million VHS/Beta machines in record mode is an essential phoneme in our new language. Likewise the breathless wheeze of the junk food joint at peak hour. The demonic DATA drumcomputer abseils our sensibilities night and day as the search for the perfect beat continues. (It happens to know where it is – underneath the Holy Grail) The emulator cunningly contrives the obsolescence of all other musical instruments, including the human voice.

The youth of Britain continue to fiddle and shout down the rest of the world despite some very nasty language problems

It's well hard, man. You what/you what? A wicked boat, it's gonna nice up England. Rallywoman. Overdrive. Wild and loose. What time is it? Fudge-packer. This is comedy. Fresh. Doom out. You don't say. No flim-flam. A right under-the-arm place. Robotron. Play it, kick it. Needs a freak. Not now, I'll tell you when. Nut! Bosh! Serious fun. Slip it to me. Cowboy. Put a sock in it. Fuck up. Tea for two. Hangups, hotdogs, slingbacks, madrags. Bad News on Tour. Pressups. Blowbacks. Relapse. Easy access, baby. Zip, snap and drop. Hurry up. Grace I know. Grace

(Marc Lebon for *i-D* magazine)

Metropolitan life has become the semiological nexus between the imaginary and 'reality'. Its increasingly cosmopolitan syntax has simultaneously extended our world and sharpened the comparative sense of the immediate, the local and the particular.

The distant hunger, poverty and misery of the Third World ('a place where nature programmes come from' (Cater, 1985), the dramatic struggle for the most basic liberties in Latin America and South Africa, rapidly travel the mass media to arrive on our TVs, in our homes. Famine in Ethiopia, massacres in the Lebanon, the Iran of the Ayatollah Khomeini: these very real differences, threatening *our* common sense and everyday experience, enter our world. They can be ignored, defused or deplored, produce anger, pity or indifference; but they are increasingly proximate. Splashed across screens and newspapers in harrowing photographs and breathless adjectives, our know-ledge of that world emerges from the signs we have at our disposal. This may do no more than set the question of how we are connected to that 'other' world temporarily evoked on the screen, but at least it does that.

The world-wide televised concert of Live Aid in 1985 was a more effective way of invading the imagination and producing money for famine victims in Ethiopia than Oxfam or reluctant government agencies. To criticize it as mere commercial hype, for failing to tackle the real sources of famine (international business, food and crop markets controlled by the same societies that produce white rock groups), is to miss its wider sense: that for the millions watching it could involve both the pleasure and passion of rock music *and* compassion and solidarity.

In less urgent transmissions, the same channels of transnational communication also permit the transfer of 'scratch', 'rap' and 'hip hop culture' from the Bronx to Brixton. The language is shared but the speech is local. London pirate radio station LWR plays US and English rap and hip hop music, while on 103.8 FM, broadcasting out of Notting Hill the Dread Broadcasting Corporation offers further black music for the city's soul and hip hop crews in their Adidas and Nike trainers, Benetton tops and £40 Pringle sweaters. In the clubs, cutting together the sounds of jazz and soul, reggae and disco, heavy metal and funk, classical and rock, a particular dialect emerges through the mixing of local black cultures, advanced technology, musical pleasure, urban aesthetics and everyday life.

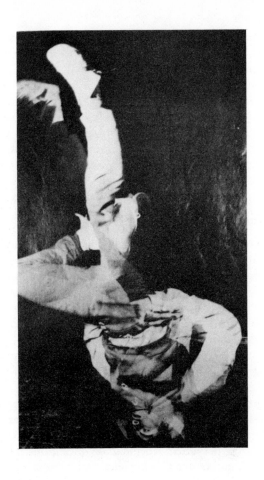

(Steve Pyke)

Trevor Birch is a B-Boy. That's 'B' for Bad, Beautiful, Black, Breaking, The Bronx. But in Trevor's case, 'B' for British. He couldn't tell you which subway line leads to the New York borough north of the Harlem river that has given him, at 18 in East London, an activity, an identity. But he has heard the records, seen the looks, knows the moves. (Rambali, 1984, 41)

The frame is common, but the local signs are distinct. Brixton or Battersea, it is not the Bronx – the investments and mix are necessarily diverse.

This, then, is the contemporary urban vernacular: the daily and tactile acceptance of existing images, languages and syntax; not as an act of resignation but as a realization of the possible, an affirmation of your right to inhabit the present.

It is an argument about popular aesthetics, about disposable culture, about everyday perception, and, ultimately, about the sense, the politics of our world.

From culture to collage

If you live in a black-and-white world, and prefer the security of an abstract utopia to the potential of the present, then contemporary popular culture merely seems to be the predictable product of capitalism and consumerism, of 'Americanization', of Britain 'going down the drain'. Yet self-righteously to castigate this culture and its forms of consumption is to miss the point. Mentally to extract ourselves from it, to turn out backs on what is actually happening, is to live an intellectual lie.

With electronic reproduction offering the spectacle of gestures, images, styles and cultures in a perpetual collage of disintegration and reintegration, the 'new' disappears into a permanent present. And with the end of the 'new' – a concept connected to linearity, to the serial prospects of 'progress', to 'modernism' – we move into a perpetual recycling of quotations, styles and fashions; an uninterrupted montage of the 'now'. The 1971 Corgi paperback cover of William Burrough's novel *The Wild Boys* becomes the 'source' of the 1984 video for the song of the same name by Duran Duran. The French critic and semiotician Roland Barthes is quoted on the pages of *New Musical Express*, the pop group Scritti Politti release a record named after a contemporary French philosopher, 'Jacques Derrida'. As the 'origins' of the signs are lost there is a consequent confusion of languages. Art and commerce, publicity and prose, are seemingly indistinguishable: is a video clip merely a commercial plug for a record or an aesthetic statement in its own right?

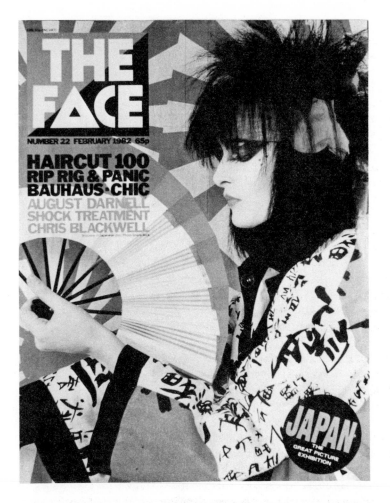

Meanwhile, the once separate historical avant-garde implodes under the pressures of this present.

In Britain, European Dadaism, Surrealism, photomontage and avant-garde cinema received a very limited acknowledgement on their appearance. Only later did they become part of a more accessible rhetoric. Under the accumulative effects of the visual and sound montage of metropolitan life, they have be-

(John Howe)

come part of the languages of today: in the design, photography, signs, logos, prose and presentation of magazines like *The Face*, *i-D* and *ZG*, in computer-aided design credits for television programmes, in certain video clips (David Bowie's 'Ashes to Ashes', Billy Ocean's 'Lover Boy'), and in the contemporary blendings of musical genres that are frequently as rich in their rapid ingenuities as the artistic research once invested in a Dada collage or avant-garde sound poem.

The sounds of unknown planets – 'Africa', 'Japan' – cross our paths, arriving out of the speakers and headphones like musical postcards. They suggest new passages through the everyday, a musical tourism amongst the sounds of the world. The

American avant-gardist composer John Cage 'scratches' the sound environment just like the black DJs in the Bronx or at London's Hip Hop Club. His project has become part of a shared perspective. Out of different histories emerges a shared habitation of common soundscapes. A Futurist manifesto – Luigi Russolo's *L'arte dei rumori* (1916) – is translated into a contemporary sound project/group: The Art of Noise on the ZTT record label, their video on *The Tube*, their LPs in the shops.

Today, the simple distinctions between low and high culture, between good and bad taste, between the profound and the super-ficial, between avant-garde and mass culture, are increasingly swamped by a wave of metropolitan connections, suggestions and sense. Different tastes, diverse artefacts, distinct forms and practices, coexist in the intertextual spaces of networks that permit both the recognition of connection and difference. Knowledge is no longer monumental and monolithic but differentiated and nomadic.

In readily accessed electronic archives, in the magnetic memory banks of records, films, tapes and videos, different cultures can be re-visited, re-vived, re-cycled, re-presented.

The corollary: contemporary 'art' is no longer the privileged field of the symbolic, of the imagination; no longer a privileged reflection on the world. It too has become an urban event, alongside television, newspapers, graffiti and pop records; a metropolitan gesture. Its previous codes are contaminated – Art becomes pop, turns profane – and pop, popular culture, acquires its own aesthetics and confuses them with the metropolitan realities of consumerism. Design, when 'the product is techni-cally outmoded it will be so aesthetically' (Banham, 1981, 92), becomes the contemporary art form *par excellence*.

This confusion and breaking of codes, this disrespect for previous authorities, boundaries and rules, also exposes what was previously subordinate and hidden. Different histories become available, their languages drawn into a contemporary eclecticism – producing unexpected encounters in the record grooves, on the dance floor, in fashion, in front of the television, in the city, and in everyday life. Almost anyone can buy these

codes, use them, wear them, hear them, see them, walk and move amongst them, live them.

Here the urban machine is no longer the privileged focus of alienation. Rather, it has become the principal means of language. The signs are used and urban space domesticated.

Take the city soundscapes that we inhabit in an increasingly familiar manner: the portable record player, the transistor radio, the car stereo, the boogie box, the Walkman . . . increasingly miniaturized and personalized they lead to individual 'urban strategies'.

Inside this mobile collage a democracy of aesthetic and cultural populism becomes possible. The previous authority of culture, once respectfully designated with a capital C, no longer has an exclusive hold on meaning. 'High culture' becomes just one more subculture, one more option, in our midst. This forces a self-conscious reassessment in the recognition of what passes for contemporary knowledge; a posterior situation to the previous intellectual disdain for, and critical distance from, 'mass culture' and popular tastes.

(David Johnson)

One experiences *walk'n'listen*, or even walk'n'eat'n'drink-'n'play'n' . . . 'n' listen (boy with roller skates eating McDonald, drinking Coke, and listening to Michael Jackson through Walkman). The pleasure of Walkman . . . can be found in the way that listening is incidentally overlapped by and mixed up with different acts: as a listening act, it is not exclusive but inclusive, not concentrated but distracted, not convergent but divergent, not centripetal but centrifugal. (Hosokawa, 1984, 176)

195

Metropolis now!

Today, the metaphysical separation between ideas and material, between original and derivative, production and reproduction, taste and commerce, culture and industry, has collapsed. The struggle over 'Culture' may still be staged – at least in the universities, learned journals, art galleries, official cultural agencies, 'serious' literature, cinema, journalism and television – between these assumed oppositions. But popular culture has bypassed the question. It is popular culture – its tastes, practices and aesthetics – that today dominates the urban scene, offering sense where traditional culture can usually only see nonsense. 'Nonsense', as the French critic Gilles Deleuze points out, invariably represents an overabundance of sense, not its absence (Deleuze, 1969).

Close up, each city dissolves into the diversified sprawl and powerful everyday realities of residential areas, shopping centres, slums, suburbia and satellite towns. For protected suburban livers, distant from the inner-city zones of increasing poverty and neglect, city centres are often little more than offices, department stores, traffic, fast food outlets, entertainment venues and parking meters.

But this does not obliterate the mythology of the seductive 'other', does not remove the 'city' from the imagination. Youth cultures continue to construct bridges, even if only courtesy of the late-night bus, to metropolitan imagery, to the place where the sounds, styles and people 'are happening'. And then there is also shopping 'in town', gambling, drinking, pool, dancing, club music, club sex; over the rich, messy, daily textures of these tastes and pleasures hangs the romantic imagery, the hidden promise of the 'bright lights, big city'.

Certainly, the city is already an object of nostalgia, the site of the imaginary, of visual, literary and intellectual aesthetization. Here the world is doubled and dislocated. In it we discover the pleasure of modern icons and modern ruins; a living museum of architectural, sartorial, musical and entertainment styles. Attentive to the hyper-realism of a sign-saturated world, we appreciate what before was hidden under the label of the 'banal' or 'superficial': those deferred histories of urban life that can be traced in the detailed changes in design and dress, sights and sounds.

(David Johnson)

Here there is no external authority to bestow sense and 'meaning' on the objects and images of our attention. The 'metropolis has no "outside"' (Rella, 1984). The histories are inscribed inside the cultural body. Meaning is concentrated here, in the profane exchange between signs and sense; culture no longer appeals to a superior truth: that 'God is dead' (Friedrich Nietzsche).

At this point, without the security of external guarantees, we find ourselves walking a narrow line between the enlargement of meaning and the peril of it breaking down and evaporating all together. It produces an 'intensification of the critical condition' (Foss, 1984); and brings us to the final chapter.

11 THEORETICAL EXPOSURES: FRAMING CULTURE

Up to now I have not introduced an explicit theoretical model or map of popular culture. I preferred first to try and evoke some of its textures; to suggest not only ways of thinking about music, the city, cinema, and everyday life, but also ways of thinking with them.

Of course no account is innocent: the interested reader can easily follow up the indications, notes and references in the previous pages to uncover the implicit route I have followed. Now, however, I want briefly to expose the structure of thinking that lies behind this book by locating it in the intellectual formation of the study of culture and popular culture in Britain over the last thirty years.

Native encounters

Thirty years ago in Britain the study of popular culture did not exist. You gained knowledge of it through direct experience: watching commercial television, sporting tight trousers and your hair in a 'DA', drinking at the 'local', listening to pop music, sipping a *cappuccino* in a newly opened coffee bar, wearing jeans and cosmetics, reading the *Daily Mirror* and *News of the World*. For a less visceral, more mediated, encounter there were the successful 'working-class' novels and films of the day: *Saturday Night and Sunday Morning*, *Room at the Top*, and Colin MacInnes's *Absolute Beginners*. But popular culture as an object of study, as something of intellectual and theoretical interest, did not exist.

Actually, that is not quite true. Although until recently it has been usually overlooked, there existed an important reflection on popular culture in Britain from the early 1950s onwards. This was developed in the area of the visual arts, in architecture, design and Pop Art at the ICA (Institute of Contemporary Arts) by the Independent Group (IG). In fact, the very term 'Pop Art', coined by the art critic Lawrence Alloway in the early 1950s, was intended to describe not a new movement in painting but the products of popular culture. 'Subjects of the IG in the 1954–55 season included: Banham on car styling (Detroit and sex symbolism); the Smithsons on the real dreams of ads versus architectural ideals; Richard Hamilton on consumer goods; and Frank Cordell on popular music (he actually made it)' (Alloway, 1966, 32).

The fact that it was not literary based, was fascinated by everyday objects, and had a lot of approving things to say about post-war, often US-derived, commercial popular culture probably explains its absence from most critical accounts.[1] And yet, in the apparently frivolous modernity of British Pop Art there existed a discourse of unacknowledged sophistication.

Within the academic world a far more tentative opening towards popular culture was inaugurated in 1957 with the publication of Richard Hoggart's highly influential book, *The Uses of Literacy*. Hoggart's work, written from 'inside' a working-class childhood in Leeds in the 1930s, drew attention, sometimes nostalgically, to the vibrant 'springs of action' in urban working-class culture. Frequently apprehensive of contemporary change, and largely blind and deaf to the potential of new forms of popular choice, American detective stories and pop music, for example, Hoggart nevertheless successfully established the popular sense of detail and immediacy, if not

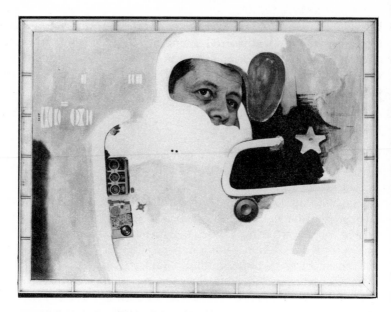

Richard Hamilton, **Towards a Definitive Statement on the Coming Trends in Men's Wear and Accessories: a) Together let us explore the Stars** (Tate Gallery, London)

We speak for convenience about a mass audience but it is a fiction. The audience today is numerically dense but highly diversified. Just as the wholesale use of subception techniques in advertising is blocked by the different perception capacities of the members of any audience, so the mass media cannot reduce everybody to one drugged faceless consumer. Fear of the Amorphous Audience is fed by the word 'mass'. In fact, audiences are specialized by age, sex, hobby, occupation, mobility, contacts, etc. Although the interests of different audiences may not be rankable in the curriculum of the traditional educational-ists, they nevertheless reflect and influence the diversification which goes with increased industrialization. It is not the hand-craft culture which offers a wide choice of goods and services to everybody (teenagers, Mrs Exeter, voyeurs, cyclists), but the industrialized one. As the market gets

bigger consumer choice increases: shopping in London is more diverse than in Rome; shopping in New York more diverse than in London. General Motors mass-produce cars according to individual selections of extras and colours. (Alloway, 1959, 42)

always the tastes, of what he called 'the full rich life'.

Raymond Williams's *Culture and Society 1780–1950*, published the following year, reached the similar conclusion that culture represented a 'whole way of life'. Williams's own project was ambitious: to analyse the concept of 'culture' and to give an account of its historical formation. Examining novelists like Dickens and D. H. Lawrence, and critics as diverse as Arnold, Ruskin, Eliot and Orwell, he identified and reconstructed a complex native debate on 'culture and society'.

Both writers, almost inevitably given their professional backgrounds, concentrated their analyses on literary texts and an associated moral seriousness which, at least in England, has tended to stand in for the more abstract criteria of Continental historiography, sociology and Marxism. What was new lay in their willingness to extend textual analysis to the previously excluded artefacts of popular taste, although they were always careful here to draw a line between jazz, football and gardening as the acceptable face of popular culture, and horror films, 'juke box boys', and 'sex-and-violence novels' as unacceptable (Hoggart, 1958; Williams, 1961).

These two books each established that the study of popular culture could not be divorced from the wider dynamic of culture as a sphere of economic, social and symbolic activity.[2] By the late 1950s, under the impact of press and publishing empires, advertising, cinema, television and the record industry, it was quite clear that the *whole* realm of contemporary culture was subject to complex social and economic conditions. The study of culture could no longer be reduced to an aesthetic or moral question but involved a 'whole way of life', a complex, lived-in 'structure of feelings' (Raymond Williams).

Swap the wooden chairs for 'tubular chairs' and the young men in the above photograph are ready for condemnation in a Hoggart vignette:

The young men waggle one shoulder or stare, as desperately as Humphrey Bogart, across the tubular chairs . . . their clothes, their hair-styles, their facial expressions all indicate . . . living to a large extent in a myth-world compounded of a few simple elements which they take to be those of American life. (Hoggart, 1958, 204)

This is quite clearly the 'bad' side of popular culture.

Structures, mythologies and signs exist . . .

To accept these premises, and, in particular, to study an area – popular culture – that they had rarely considered, except negatively, which had grown without their authority and in which they had virtually no part to play, has not proved easy for many intellectuals. It is what the French sociologist Edgar Morin once called a 'monumental displacement'.[3]

One possibility was to approach it obliquely, by stretching tried methods to cover this previously ignored area: i.e. the literary-critical method pioneered by F. R. Leavis and *Scrutiny* magazine in the 1930s of a 'close' and sensitive 'reading' of the 'lived' or 'felt' experiences of a 'community' and a 'tradition'.[4] This was the approach adopted and extended by Hoggart and Williams.

Another approach was to use a seemingly neutral methodology and examine how the object – whether a novel, advertisement or television show – was structured, and to discover in its structure a cultural semantics. Like a language, a limited set of combinatory rules is able to generate an infinite set of statements. This is true whether we are talking about a Bach fugue, a fairy story or fashion. The structuralist approach therefore broke through the limits of more traditional literary criticism by permitting a common treatment of the most heterogeneous objects and practices: from the myths of South American Indians to the advert for a soap powder and reading Marx. It was developed mainly in France in the 1950s and 1960s, and was widely associated with Claude Lévi-Strauss, Roland Barthes and Louis Althusser.[5]

The structuralist analysis of culture led to a questioning of the existing distinctions between literature and social anthropology, between sociology and history. In Britain it provided an important impetus to an inter-disciplinary approach – 'cultural studies' – that, drawing initially on the work of Hoggart and Williams, was largely pioneered by the Centre for Contemporary Cultural Studies, Birmingham, under the directorship of Stuart Hall.

But it was not until the early 1970s, after the rise of the 'New

Left' and the wave of student unrest and radical politics that had swept Western Europe and the United States, that structuralism came to be considered an appropriate methodology. In an intellectual climate now tuned to establishing wider commitments and 'positions', it challenged the previous vagaries of an unsystematic pragmatism and the localized positivism of native sociology. The everyday quality of Hoggart's details and the vagueness of concepts such as 'culture', although Williams was already gesturing towards Marxism and the fact that 'it is capitalism . . . which is confusing us' (Williams, 1961, 327), no longer provided sufficient explanatory force.

One native response was E. P. Thompson's *The Making of the English Working Class* (1968). This monumental, Marxist history was informed by the rich cultural dynamism (the 'making') that connnected 'social being' to 'social consciousness', and insisted, against Williams's formulation, on the study of a 'whole way of *struggle*'. But a wider, more methodological response also existed elsewhere. Where was the 'motor' that drove social details and concepts into synthesis, what transformed an idea of culture into a dynamic structure, what made it a lived experience that could be related to society as a whole? The reply lay in the terms set by the question: synthesis, structure, society as a whole: 'totality'.

Explanations based on the idea of totality, on the rational frame that connects the most distant and complex parts, are characteristic of the great Continental schools of thought. We find it in all the major intellectual systems of modernity: Marxism, classical sociology, psychoanalysis, structuralism, semiology.[6]

Although initially drawing upon an assumed parallel between the structure of the human mind and the structure of its cultures (Lévi-Strauss), the mechanisms that were more frequently revealed in structuralist analysis were the 'mythologies' of the contemporary world (Barthes, 1973). The analyst reveals what lies behind appearances, names that which avoids being named: ideology, the bourgeoisie, capitalism. The analyst seeks to demonstrate that the everyday world is not chaotic but constructed, is not given but structured. Looking at literature,

206

television, advertising or fashion, the purpose of structuralist analysis was to investigate their signs in an attempt to restore a de-mythologized, political truth. It set out to demonstrate, defuse and demystify the mechanisms of distorted representations (ideology); it sought by exposing their structures to re-politicize their languages.

This eventually opens up the path towards a cultural semiotics: 'reading' culture as a political struggle over language. Whether we are talking of the languages of literature, fashion, cinema, comics or design, it became appropriate to examine them for signs of resistance, and to trace in their syntax an ideological struggle. One of the most notable examples of this type of analysis in Britain has been the Birmingham Centre's work on male working-class subcultures. Customized motor bikes and scooters, a seemingly fanatical concern with details of dress and hair, and allegiance to particular (usually imported) musics, provided a series of obvious examples drawn from British youth cultures. Here the assumed rules of the languages of transport, fashion and commercial music have been broken, interrupted, scrambled . . . resisted.[7]

Reading the signs of youth subcultures, the analysts found in them the stylistically mediated symbols of class. Homologies between the housing estate, a dead-end job, Brylcreemed hair, a crinoline skirt and a Presley record, were suggested as an imaginary solution to social and cultural subordination. However, although that was undoubtedly an important step, the more recent rhetoric of subcultural insubordination has suggested less direct, more complex connections and contexts. Since punk confused the signs of music and dress in its self-parodying, media-conscious collage we have learnt that the social metaphors a subculture employs (its choice of music, clothes, drugs – its 'style') can rarely be reduced to a single or unambiguous source.[8]

Youth subcultures are extremely public and spectacular signs. What of those languages that are altogether more silent? How do we locate signs of resistance, what the Italian semiotician Umberto Eco once called 'semiotic guerrilla warfare', in the television audience of *EastEnders*, amongst readers of *Cosmopolitan* and *Mizz*, or in the quiet style of a Cecil Gee suit? The

MAIL ORDER

The first fissures in the analysis – challenging the male principle: the questioning of his meaning, his construct, his order and his explanation. **In documenting the temporary flights of the Teds, Mods or Rockers . . . they fail to show that it is monstrously more difficult for women to escape (even temporarily) and that these symbolic flights have often been at the expense of women (especially mothers) and girls. The lads may get by with – and get off on – each other alone on the streets but they did not eat, sleep or make love there.** (McRobbie, 1980, 40)

208

programme, magazine or item of clothing is not simply an ideological statement to be accepted or denied; its possible meanings are not exhausted by ideology; it rarely offers a straightforward example of obvious incorporation or resistance.

A more subtle understanding of the relation between ideology and meaning, class and culture, eventually emerged with the sophisticated sense of 'structure' elaborated in the work of the French Marxist philosopher Louis Althusser in the 1960s. In place of the Marxian idea of a mechanical or causal structure,

The Birmingham Centre for Contemporary Cultural Studies had already opened an important and fruitful dialogue with Continental theory, re-examining the meaning and action concerns of earlier European sociology (Weber, Durkheim, Dilthey and Schutz), and critically adopting some of the more recent structuralist arguments of Lévi-Strauss, Barthes and Althusser. And it was collective work and studies developed in Birmingham that did much to develop ideological analyses during the 1970s, including the eventual adoption of the more sophisticated idea of 'hegemony'.[9]

where the economic basis of society (the 'base') is assumed directly to determine political and cultural life (the 'superstructures'), Althusser proposed a structure of effects: the 'effectivity of a structure on its elements'. The complex interaction between economic, political and cultural forces produces a rich, 'overdetermined' reality. There are no automatic or mechanical connections between the different forces and relations, but a complexly determined situation or 'conjuncture' that is historically specific (Althusser and Balibar, 1970). What is important here is that this more complex idea of structure and determination provoked some important rethinking about the idea of ideology.

. . . in and through each of us

The concept of 'ideology' was extensively developed by Karl Marx and subsequent Marxism to explain the unconscious mechanisms that bind different social subjects, divided by wealth and class (with the more recent acknowledgement that gender and race are also involved in the construction of the ideological 'subject') into a common society. Ideology continually papers over these cracks in the social fabric as it works to prevent obvious social and economic inequalities from spilling over into open confrontation.

Ideology is therefore a process that seeks pacifically to transform a particular distribution of powers, choices and directions into appearing 'natural', 'fair', and 'normal'; into appearing as simply the expression of a shared 'common sense': the 'only' or 'best thing to do' in the circumstances. It is the successful installation of this common frame of reference in the institutions and experiences of daily life – at home, on television, in the press, in the curriculum and culture of the school, at work, in political parties, religious organizations and trade unions – that the Italian Marxist Antonio Gramsci called 'hegemony'. Under hegemony, ideology is not directly imposed but continually composed through a mobile strategy of shifting alliances and compromises formed in pursuit of a government by 'consensus'.

Ideology, then, is not something imposed from 'above', but

continually works in and through each of us. It provides the daily plasma in which we cohere, recognize our 'selves', and move and act as unified subjects. To contest it and demonstrate that there can be other views, other choices and possibilities, also means that we have to contest our inherited 'selves'. This investigation of the 'I' has been long established as the province of psychoanalysis. It was psychoanalysis, in particular the attention of the French psychoanalyst Jacques Lacan to how we enter the representative mechanisms of language and become subjects (recognize our selves as an 'I'), that has recently led to some important extensions in understanding the profoundly unconscious nature of ideology. Subsequently translated into a Marxist lexicon by Althusser, the contesting of how we are constructed, represented and recognized has since been most fruitfully explored in the discussion and practices of the visual representations of sexuality, particularly by feminists.[10]

Between the Gramscian concept of 'hegemony' and research on the formation of the 'subject', ideology could no longer be considered simply to be the distorted reflection of a static, singular power such as 'capitalism', or the 'bourgeoisie'; something merely to be unmasked by the mythologist. It now occupied a dynamic role in the production and reproduction of those and other powers inside social, sexed and individual formations. Here, ideology becomes a flexible co-ordinator, and comes close to Michel Foucault's work on the local organization of knowledge and power: the 'discourse' where relations, objects and subjects are positioned according to the unfolding strategy of 'micro-powers' exercised by a particular practice: the discourse of the clinic, of the prison, of sexuality.[11]

Inside the signs: meaning goes mobile

Since the mid-1970s, the concepts of ideology, hegemony, the subject and discourse have all played a major role in cultural analyses.[12] But the problem with the ideological critique of culture, society and its products is that if we are all wrapped up in ideology, subjects of a discourse, what purpose can the knowledge of our ideological construction serve if we can never escape from it? Once we have diagnosed our state how can we change it?

If ideology is all around us, inscribed in our clothes, our homes, hair styles, reading and viewing habits; in our gestures, our sexuality, our selves, then we can no longer measure resistence and the struggle for change along the yardstick of a non-ideological reality: that existential moment of assumed 'authenticity' which contests the 'false' world of ideological appearances. Change and transformation can no longer be considered as something to be injected into the 'false' world from elsewhere. It must now involve a question of inflection, emphasis and direction inside the continuing constructions of everyday experience and the conditions we inherit. This suggests a revision in the idea of cultural resistance and sign warfare.

It becomes necessary, as the French critic Jacques Derrida has consistently argued in his objections to structuralism, to play with the signs, to explore the languages that apparently 'subject' us. We need to disrupt the presumed coherence of ideology, texts and images – the world of representations in which we come to recognize our social and sexual 'selves' – and rediscover the details of the bits that go into their making. That means living inside the signs. It means engaging in the contradictory pleasures of fashion, style, television soap, video games, sport, shopping, reading, drinking, sexuality. Here, meaning and pleasure, politics and aesthetics, are no longer tied to an abstract morality injected from 'outside', but to the knowledge of inhabiting the signs of the contemporary world. Extending our knowledge through these details and their sense of the possible, the previous totality of sense offered by ideology (including Marxism) is 'deconstructed', and its elements relocated in a more detailed, more complex, more specific and more open (i.e. transforming and transformable) perspective.[13]

The model of analysis changes. We can no longer overlook the heterogeneous surface activities of everyday life, they too are real. It is there that signs and representations (whether writing or advertising, photography or pornography) are encountered, inhabited and invested with sense. So, to explain them by

212

simply referring to the logic of a deep structure or the mechanisms of a totality, where 'any reality, once described is struck off the inventory' (Jean-Paul Sartre), invariably privileges the mechanical and the reductive. A horizontal vista of mobile meanings, shifting connections, temporary encounters, a world of inter-textual richness and detail, needs to be inserted into the critical model. Complexity needs to be respected. There is a knowledge connected to the internal axes of structures. And there is a knowledge that moves over the surface and requires the horizontal reading associated with maps. Between the two we can plot a changing body of sense.

The 'dense and concrete' life

So, in a roundabout way, and with a wider horizon, we return to the details of that 'dense and concrete' life that Richard Hoggart passionately discussed some three decades ago.

The recent crisis and defensive hardening of certain intellectual models that have contributed to the formation of cultural analyses, in particular those of Marxist origin, can, paradoxically, also be read as the positive effect of the power of the previously unspoken entering the languages of the present: 'a situation in which we feel an accumulation of energies that go beyond the saturated conventions and rules which at one time coincided with the extremes of our awareness' (Gargani, 1979).

This crisis in the exhaustive/exhausted model, where developments, forces and tendencies seemingly slip beyond a previous rationality and intellectual control ('criticism' is, of course, etymologically connected to 'crisis'), throws the philosophical distance of the intellectual into play. In critical modes of enquiry, the return to the (theoretically informed) specific and the detailed has increasingly cut across the personal as well as the professional dimensions of life. It was significantly the development of feminism in the 1970s that simultaneously drew these dimensions together and threatened the totalizing explanation of existing social, cultural and political rationalities.

With the emergence of a previously silenced language, a hidden history, an earlier truth is challenged. Other histories, other knowledges, other dimensions and details, break in upon former perspectives. Intellectual work that is sensitive to the present is forced to recognize its limits, its partiality, its own precariousness.[14] No longer the summation of knowledge or culture, it offers a particular force in a world where there are no immediate guarantees. Seeking and suggesting connections in an acknowledge complexity, it sets the terms for what Jean-François Lyotard has recently called a 'new materialism'.

A final note: is this the end?

The price paid by a powerful rationality is a terrific limitation in the objects it manages to see and can talk about. (Vattimo and Rovatti, 1983)

Recently in the Anglo-Saxon world a series of theoretical skirmishes have taken place between the older, rationalist, in-depth model of totality and a newer, effervescent, flat theory, between, to use the terms employed, 'modernism' and 'post-

214

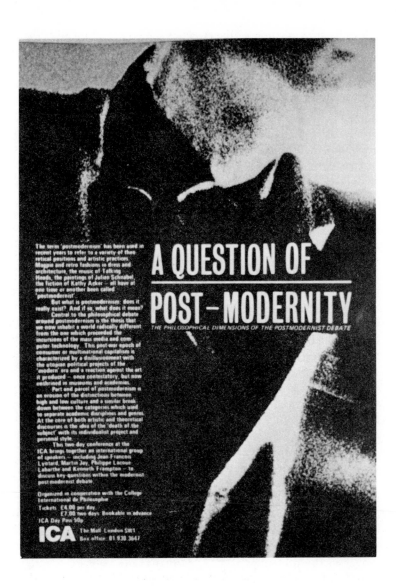

The term 'postmodernism' has been used in
recent years to refer to a variety of theoretical positions and artistic practices.
Magpie and retro fashions in dress and
architecture, the music of Talking
Heads, the paintings of Julian Schnabel,
the fiction of Kathy Acker – all have at
one time or another been called
'postmodernist'.

But what is postmodernism: does it
really exist? And if so, what does it mean?

Central to the philosophical debate
around postmodernism is the thesis that
we now inhabit a world radically different
from the one which preceded the
invention of the mass media and computer technology. This post-war epoch of
consumer or multinational capitalism is
characterized by a disillusionment with
the utopian political project of the
'modern' era and a reaction against the art
it produced – once contestatory, but now
enshrined in museums and academies.

Part and parcel of postmodernism is
an erosion of the distinctions between
high and low culture and a similar break
down between the categories which used
to separate academic disciplines and genres.
At the core of both artistic and theoretical
discourses is the idea of the 'death of the
subject' with its individualist project and
personal style.

This two-day conference at the
ICA brings together an international group
of speakers – including Jean-François
Lyotard, Martin Jay, Philippe Lacoue-
Labarthe and Kenneth Frampton – to
discuss key questions within the modernist
post-modernist debate.

Organized in cooperation with the Collège
International de Philosophie

Tickets £4.00 per day.
£7.00 two days Bookable in advance
ICA Day Pass 50p

ICA The Mall London SW1
Box office 01 930 3647

A QUESTION OF
POST – MODERNITY
THE PHILOSOPHICAL DIMENSIONS OF THE POSTMODERNIST DEBATE

moderism': a 'war of the worlds' between two apparently separate semantic planets (Hebdige, 1985).

What is important in all this in the context of this book, is how, among its many aspects, the debate over post-modernism can also be read as the symptom of the disruptive ingression of popular culture, its aesthetics and intimate possibilities, into a previously privileged domain. Theory and academic discourses are confronted by the wider, unsystematized, popular networks of cultural production and knowledge. The intellectual's privilege to explain and distribute knowledge is threatened; his authority, for it is invariably 'his', redimensionalized. This in part explains both the recent defensiveness of the modernist, particularly Marxist, project, and the cold nihilism of certain notorious strands in post-modernism.[15]

For if an intellectual will can reduce *all* social, cultural and political life to the reductive mechanics of 'class struggle', it can equally transform them into Baudrillard's negative sociology of the sign invasion of the world where differences are reduced to indifference and we all become objects of a meaningless and uncontrollable semiotics: anonymous actors invoked by 'an immense script and a perpetual motion picture' (Baudrillard 1983a, 26). But in neither case can the particular rationality employed presume to speak for the forces it indicates. This waking up from the rationalist dream of total intelligibility ('rationalism is not the highest point of reason', Gianni Vattimo), no matter whether you choose to get out on the modernist or post-modernist side of the bed, invariably produces the melancholy language of resignation, closure and apocalypse.

But meaning does not die in intellectual despair, or disappear into a theoretical black hole. Outside the study the world continues to turn. The debate over modernism/post-modernism is ultimately the sign (deferred, displaced, denied . . .) of a debate over the changed politics of knowledge, authority and power in the present world. A particular mode of explaining, including that of the post-modernist prophet who announces the 'end of meaning' but significantly refuses to relinquish the right to speak incessantly of that 'end', is now supplemented and decentred by the more extensive semantics of a socialized collage.

The world has moved on. It is no longer necessarily tied to traditional discourses, institutions and voices for information about its meaning. The centres of history have multiplied, both internally and externally. Even white, ex-colonial Europe sometimes seems a self-obsessed, fashionable ruin on the sidelines of tomorrow's world: Africa, Latin America, the East, Japan, the shores of the Pacific.

It is in the invariably rich, expanded, and sometimes cruel complexity of this everyday world, as I hope this book has illustrated, that choices, sentiments, hopes, desires, tastes, meanings, histories, theories and politics are expressed and pursued. It is there, in the detailed texture of its relations and practices, that we encounter different powers and different knowledges which introduce us through diverse signs, languages and machinery to the potential of a detailed popular order; that is, a politics of the possible.

Notes

1. This discourse can be recovered by reading Alloway's important 1959 essay, 'The Long Front of Culture' (1959), Alloway (1966), the Banham collection (1981), and Hebdige (1983).

2. Subsequently reinforced with the publication of Williams's *The Long Revolution* (1961); and Stuart Hall's and Paddy Whannell's *The Popular Arts* (1964).

3. This comes from Morin's own excellent pioneering and anti-pessimistic analysis of contemporary popular culture, *L'esprit du temps* (1962), which, rather symptomatically, was not translated into English.

4. For a detailed discussion of *Scrutiny* in its European context and for its role in establishing so many of the concerns that have dominated subsequent English and cultural studies, see Mulhern (1979).

5. Structuralism was by no means only a Parisian phenomenon. Apart from its debt to linguistics (Saussure, Jakobson, Chomsky),

contemporary schools of structuralism, and their subsequent transformation into semiology or semiotics (the 'science of signs'), were conspicuously present in both Italy and the Soviet Union. However, it was overwhelmingly French structuralism and semiology that was to be absorbed and recycled in Britain.

6. For a detailed discussion of the impact and effects of Continental sociology and structuralism on the project of cultural studies and theories of 'knowledge', see Hall (1977).

7. See the work of the Birmingham Centre for Contemporary Cultural Studies (*Resistance through Rituals*, 1976), and its subsequent revision and extension in the brilliant 'reading' offered by Dick Hebdige in *Subculture: The Meaning of Style* (1979). For an important criticism of the 'masculine' bias of such studies, see McRobbie (1980).

8. In fact the very knowledge of ideology inscribed in the image can eventually be re-incorporated in the cultural and semantic play of the object and subsequent style (particularly in the self-knowing contexts of 'camp'). See chapter 7.

9. On cultural analysis, ideology and hegemony, and its application to particular histories, see the collectively produced volumes of the Centre for Contemporary Cultural Studies published by Hutchinson since 1976 – *Resistance through Rituals*, *Women Take Issue*, *On Ideology*, *Working Class Culture*, *Culture*, *Media*, *Language*, *Unpopular Education*, *Making Histories*, *The Empire Strikes Back* – along with *Policing the Crisis* (1978), also written by members of the Centre, and Paul Willis, *Learning to Labour* (1977). Hall (1980) provides a useful summary of the emergence of these themes in the context of the Centre's own history. Since Stuart Hall left the Centre in 1979 work has continued under the directorship of Richard Johnson.

10. The subsequent extension of the analysis of the ideological 'subject' through a psychoanalytically (Lacanian) inflected semiotics was largely introduced into Britain from France by the theoretical film magazine *Screen*. For an excellent overview, see Tickner (1984).

11. For an introduction to these ideas, see the first chapter of Foucault (1979). Foucault's attention to the *internal* distribution of power and knowledge in a particular field is not immediately

assimilable to Gramsci's altogether wider analysis of the complex passage of 'hegemony', where a 'decisive economic nucleus' becomes 'party' to the organization and leadership of society as a whole (Gramsci 1971).

12. Apart from the above-mentioned work of the CCCS, see the Open University Popular Culture course, U203 (1982); for cinema and television, see past numbers of *Screen Education* (sadly defunct) and *Screen*; for literary studies, see Williams (1977), Widdowson (1982) and Eagleton (1983).

13. This shift invokes the authority of two nineteenth-century fathers: Marx and Nietzsche. The criticism of rationalism's faith in the ability of reason, dialectics and the 'philosophy of history' to reveal fully the mechanisms of society, has been contested by French post-structuralist and post-modernist critics: Deleuze, Barthes, Foucault, Derrida, Baudrillard. Drawing upon Friedrich Nietzsche's sceptical deconstruction of the rationalist belief in an exhaustive explanation of society and history arrived at through abstract reason and logic, the very idea of 'totality' is shown to be a metaphysics which tries to master reality by force. Nietzsche's objections are directed against the hegemonic Western (Platonic) philosophic tradition that has regularly drawn a neat distinction between explaining an 'authentic' world and separating it from false appearances. But can reason confidently extract itself from the world of appearances (the dream of a Marxist 'science'), or is it so implicated in the conditions it seeks to describe that its results can only be provisional, open-ended, still to be validated? Put another way, can 'liberation' or 'freedom' actually exist outside or beyond appearances? For a useful summary, see the chapter 'Between Marx and Nietzsche: the politics of deconstruction', in Norris (1982).

14. Recently a group of Italian philosophers have argued through the 'crisis of reason' and the 'end of the metaphysical adventure' for the limits of rationality to be inscribed in intellectual work. This results in a provisional 'weak thought' that does not presume to speak in the name of a totalizing model, truth or authority (Vattimo and Rovatti, 1983). For an introduction to this important contribution, so far largely

overlooked in the Anglo-Saxon world, see Chambers and Curti (1982).

15. For Marxist objections to post-modernism, objections which sometimes also include modernism, see Anderson (1984) and Latimer (1984). Anderson's criticisms are largely directed against the detailed but inoffensive historical study of modernism by Marshall Berman (1983). For useful introductions to post-modernism, see Frankovits (1984), Jameson (1984), Lyotard (1984), the issue of *New German Critique*, n. 33 (1984) devoted to the issue, and Foster (1985). A taste of the complete dissolution of meaning that leaves us blankly observing the growing 'desert of the real', can be sampled in Baudrillard (1983a, 1983b, 1985). For a carefully argued position from within an English intellectual formation, see Hebdige (1985).

Suggestions for further work

1. In contemporary culture, 'simple distinctions between low and high culture, between good and bad taste, between the profound and the superficial, between avant-garde and mass culture, are increasingly swamped by a wave of metropolitan connections, suggestions and sense' (see p. 192).
Why? Give some examples.

2. Eduardo Paolozzi speaking in 1958:
It is conceivable that in 1958 a higher order of imagination exists in a SF pulp produced in the outskirts of L.A. than (in) the little (literary) magazine of today. Also it might be possible that sensations of a difficult-to-describe nature be expended at the showing of a low-budget horror film. Does the modern artist consider this? (In Alloway, 1966)
Along with the modern artist, we could extend Paolozzi's question by adding critics and intellectuals. Why, in your opinion, did most British intellectuals choose to ignore or disparage popular culture in the 1950s and '60s, or, if sympathetic, usually treat it with such caution?

3. Compared to the native method of a 'close reading' what advantage lay in studying contemporary society as a structured reality and as a sign system?

4. Indicate the advances made in cultural studies by ideological analysis, and whether it in turn poses a further series of problems.

5. On the front page of *The Sunday Times* of 1 September 1985 there was a Harrod's advertisement for a new range of female 'Dynasty style' clothes:

All the glamour of 'Dynasty' is here. Nolan Miller, designer for the series has now created a collection for off-screen appearances.

This provides a neat caption to Baudrillard's idea that signs have totally invaded and occupied everyday life. However, without denying the fundamental change in experience that has taken place in this mediated world, we might want to object to Baudrillard's totalizing vision. Try and suggest what are the limits and consequences of the proposal that we are merely actors and actresses in an uncontrollable sign play.

FURTHER MATERIALS

Videos

Cool Cats, MGM/UA.
Girl Groups: The Story of a Sound, MGM/UA.
Hip-Hop, A Street History, PGV.
Ready, Steady, Go!, Vols 1, 2 & 3, PMI.
The Other Side of Nashville, MGM/UA.
Legend – The Best of Bob Marley and The Wailers, Island.
The Great Rock'n'Roll Swindle, Virgin.
Death Valley Days: Four Track Scratch EP, Gorilla Tapes. (This is
   an example of video scratching.)

Records

The selection below follows the histories presented in chapters 7–9 and is largely limited to albums that offer a 'slice' of a particular sound or era. For a more detailed discography, particularly for post-1950 pop music, see Chambers (1985).

The Golden Age of Music Hall, RHA.

The Original Dixieland Jazz Band, EMI.
This is Henry Hall, EMI.
Presenting The Golden Age of the Hollywood Musical, UAG.
Benny Goodman: A Legendary Performer, RCA.
Vera Lynn: Hits of the Blitz, EMI.
The Very Best of Frank Sinatra, EMI.

Hank Williams, *40 Greatest Hits*, Polydor.

The Scott Joplin Ragtime Album, CBS.
The Story of the Blues, vols 1 & 2, CBS.
Billie Holliday, *The Golden Years*, vols 1 and 2, CBS.
Duke Ellington, *Ellington at Newport*, CBS.
Count Basie, *Blues I Love to Sing*, Ace of Hearts.
Charlie Parker, *Quintet of the Year*, Debut/Vogue.
Miles Davis, *Kind of Blue*, CBS.
John Coltrane, *Coltrane*, Impulse.
Archie Shepp, *Mama Too Tight*, Impulse.
Albert Ayler, *Reevaluations: The Impulse Years*, Impulse.
Ornette Coleman, *Free Jazz*, Atlantic.
T-Bone Walker, *T-Bone Jumps Again*, Charly.
The Best of Muddy Waters, Chess.
The Best of B. B. King, Anchor.
Bo Diddley, *Golden Decade*, Chess.
Fats Domino, *20 Greatest Hits*, United Artists.

The Iron Muse: A Panorama of Industrial Folk Music, Topic.
Sea Songs and Shanties, TPS.
The Joan Baez File, Pye.
Bob Dylan, *The Freewheelin' Bob Dylan*, CBS.
The Donovan File, Pye.
Bert Jansch, Transatlantic.
Judy Collins, *In My Life*, Elektra.

Alan Freed's Memory Lane, Pye.

The Best of Sun Rockabilly, vols 1 and 2, Charly.
Elvis Presley, *The Sun Collection*, RCA.
Chuck Berry, *Motivatin'*, Chess.
The Original Jerry Lee Lewis, Charly.
Buddy Holly, *20 Golden Greats*, MCA.
The Everly Brothers, *Don and Phil's Fabulous Fifties Treasury*, Phonogram.
Cliff Richard, *40 Golden Greats*, EMI.
Elvis Presley, *40 Greatest*, RCA.
Phil Spector's Greatest Hits, Impression.
Drifters, *24 Original Hits*, Atlantic.
The Four Seasons, *Greatest Hits*, K-Tel.
Golden Hits of the Shangri-Las, Philips

Leadbelly's Last Sessions, Folkways.
Woody Guthrie, *Dust Bowl Ballads*, Folkways.
The Donegan File, Pye.

The Beatles, *1962–1966*, Parlophone.
Hits of the Mersey Era, EMI.
Georgie Fame and the Blue Flames, *R'n'B at the Flamingo*, Columbia.
Rolling Stones 2, Decca.
Animals, *Most of the Animals*, Columbia.
Rolling Stones, *Aftermath*, Decca.
The Who, *The Story of the Who*, Polydor.
The Kink File, Pye.
The Beatles, *Sergeant Pepper's Lonely Hearts Club Band*, Parlophone.

Bob Dylan, *Blonde On Blonde*, CBS.
Cream, *Disraeli Gears*, Polydor.
Jimi Hendrix, *Electric Ladyland*, Polydor.
Van Morrison, *Astral Weeks*, Warner Bros.
Jefferson Airplane, *Flight Log*, RCA.
Love, *Forever Changes*, Elektra.
The Doors, *Weird Scenes Inside the Goldmine*, Elektra.
Grateful Dead, *Live Dead*, Warner Bros.
Janis Joplin, *Cheap Thrills*, CBS.
Woodstock, Atlantic.
Neil Young, *After the Goldrush*, Reprise.
Joni Mitchell, *Blue*, Reprise.
The Band, Capitol.

The Eagles, *Their Greatest Hits*, Asylum.
Chicago Transit Authority, CBS.

A 25th Anniversary in Show Business Salute to Ray Charles, Atlantic.
This is Sam Cooke, RCA.
James Brown at the Apollo. Volume 1, Polydor.
Atlantic Black Gold, Atlantic.
The Stax Story, vols 1 and 2, Stax.
The Motown Story, (5 record set), Tamla Motown.
Aretha Franklin, *Aretha's Gold*, Atlantic.
The Best of Gladys Knight and the Pips, Buddah.
James Brown, *Superbad*, Polydor.
Sly and the Family Stone, *Greatest Hits*, Epic.
Miles Davis, *Bitches Brew*, CBS.
Isaac Hayes, *Hot Buttered Soul*, Stax.
Al Green, *I'm Still In Love With You*, London.
Millie Jackson, *Caught Up*, Spring.
Chic, *Très Chic*, Atlantic.
Disco Party, Polydor.
Souled Out, K-Tel.
Saturday Night Fever, Polydor.
Parliament, *The Clones of Doctor Funkenstein*, Casablanca.
Rapped Uptight, Sugarhill.

Tighten Up, 8 volumes, Trojan.
The Harder They Come, Island.
Bob Marley and The Wailers, *Catch A Fire*, Island.
Bob Marley and The Wailers, *Burnin'*, Island.
The Front Line, Island.
Culture, *Harder Than The Rest*, Virgin.
African Dub, *Chapter 3*, Joe Gibbs
Cry Tuff Dub Encounters, Part 2/Prince Far-I in Dub, Virgin.
Tapper Zukie, *MPLA*, Klik.
Steel Pulse, *Handsworth Revolution*, Island.
Linton Kwesi Johnson, *Bass Culture*, Island.
Dennis Bovell, *Brain Damage*, Fontana.

Andy Warhol's Velvet Underground, Polydor.
David Bowie, *The Rise and Fall of Ziggy Stardust And The Spiders from Mars*, RCA.
David Bowie, *Heroes*, RCA.
Patti Smith, *Horses*, Arista.

225

The Roxy, London WC2, Harvest.
Sex Pistols, *Never Mind the Bollocks*, Virgin.
The Clash, CBS.

Bruce Springsteen, *Darkness On The Edge Of Town*, CBS.
Elvis Costello, *This Year's Model*, Radar.
The Pretenders, Sire.
The Police, *Reggatta de Blanc*, A & M.

King Sunny Ade, *Juju Music*, Island.
Let the Music Scratch, Casablanca.
Michael Jackson, *Thriller*, Epic.
Talking Heads, *Stop Making Sense*, EMI.
Keith LeBlanc & Malcolm X 'No Sell Out' (45 rpm), Tommy
  Boy.
Afrika Bambaataa, Planet Patrol, *et al.*, *The Perfect Beat*,
  Tommy Boy/Polydor.
Latin Roots, Cariño.
All Africa Radio, NME cassette 019.
Tina Turner, *Private Dancer*, Capitol.
Kid Creole and the Coconuts, *Fresh Fruits and Foreign Places*,
  Island.
Bobby Womack, *The Poet 11*, Motown.
Madonna, *Like A Virgin*, Sire.
U2, *The Unforgettable Fire*, Island.
Nona Hendryx, *The Heat*, RCA.
The Style Council, *Our Favourite Shop*, Polydor.

The British Library National Sound Archive (29 Exhibition
Road, London SW7) has over half a million records and
thousands of hours of tapes. A lot of this material consists of
popular music, including interviews, studio sessions and live
concerts. It can be consulted free of charge.

Finally, for anybody interested in teaching popular music,
whether as music or as a cultural practice, I strongly recom-
mend both Vulliamy and Lee (1982) and Fleming and Muirden
(1985).

Film and television

Many of the films mentioned regularly crop up in the TV
schedules, and others can be hired on videocassette. For the
enthusiast in search of further information there are the various

services offered by the British Film Institute (BFI Library Services, 127 Charing Cross Road, London WC2; BFI Publishing, Education and Stills Department, 81 Dean Street, London W1). For critical and theoretical discussions of cinema and television, see *Screen* and *Primetime*.

Books and magazines

Frankly, nearly all the books I would suggest I have used myself in writing this book; so, they can be found in the References. However, I would also add a regular reading of such magazines as *Block*, *Ten.8* and *Monitor* (as well as back issues of *ZG*, now apparently defunct), together with less specialized publications, in particular *The Face*.

REFERENCES

Adorno, T. W. (1973) 'Correspondence with Benjamin', *New Left Review*, 81.

Alloway, L. (1959) 'The Long Front of Culture' in Russell, J. and Gablik, S. (eds) (1969).

—— (1966) 'The Development of British Pop' in Lippard, L. (ed.) (1966).

Althusser, L. and Balibar, E. (1970) *Reading Capital*, London: New Left Books.

Anderson, P. (1984) 'Modernity and Revolution', *New Left Review*, 144.

Aspinall, S. and Murphy, R. (eds) (1983) *Gainsborough Melodrama*, London: British Film Institute.

Banham, R. (1963) 'Who is this "Pop"?' in Banham (1981).

—— (1981) *Design By Choice*, London: Academy Editions.

Barker, M. (1984) *A Haunt of Fears*, London: Pluto.

Barnes, R. (1976) *Coronation Cups and Jam Jars*, London: Centerprise Publications.

—— (1979) *Mods!*, London: Eel Pie.

Barthes, R. (1973) *Mythologies*, London: Paladin.

—— (1977) *Image-Music-Text*, London: Fontana.

—— (1981) *Camera Lucida – Reflections on Photography*, London: Cape.

Baudrillard, J. (1983a) *Simulations*, New York: Semiotext(e).

—— (1983b) *In the Shadow of the Silent Majorities*, New York: Semiotext(e).

—— (1985) 'The Ecstasy of Communication' in Foster (1985).

Beckett, A. (1968) 'Stones', *New Left Review*, 47.

Benjamin, W. (1973) 'The work of art in the age of mechanical reproduction' in *Illuminations*, London: Fontana.

Bennett, T., Boyd-Bowman, S., Mercer, C. and Woollacott, J. (eds) (1981) *Popular Television and Film*, London: BFI.

Berger, J. and Mohr, J. (1982) *Another Way of Telling*, London and New York: Writers and Readers Publishing Cooperative.

Bergman, B. (1985) *Hot Sauces: Latin and Caribbean Pop*, New York: Quill.

Berman, M. (1983) *All That Is Solid Melts Into Air*, London: Verso.

Brooks, R. (1984) 'Guys and Dolls: Clones and Doubles', *ZG*, 11.

Burgin, V. (1984) 'Something About Photographic Theory', *Screen*, vol. 25: 1.

Calabi, D. (ed.) (1982) *Architettura domestica in Gran Bretagna, 1890–1939*, Milan: Electra.

Cannadine, D. and Reeder, D. (eds) (1982) *Exploring the urban past. Essays in urban history by H. J. Dyos*, Cambridge: Cambridge University Press.

Cardiff, D. and Scannell, P. (1981) 'Radio in World War II' in unit 8 of *Popular Culture*, Milton Keynes: Open University Press.

Carter, A. (1982) *Nothing Sacred*, London: Virago.

Castells, M. (1979) *The Urban Question*, London: Arnold.

Cater, N. (1985) 'The Hungry Media', *Ten.8*, 19.

Centre for Contemporary Cultural Studies (1978) *Women Take Issue*, London: Hutchinson.

—— (1978) *On Ideology*, London: Hutchinson.

—— (1981) *Unpopular Education: Schooling and social democracy in England since 1944*, London: Hutchinson.

—— (1982) *Making Histories: Studies in history-writing and politics*, London: Hutchinson.

—— (1982) *The Empire Strikes Back: Race and racism in 70s Britain*, London: Hutchinson.

Chambers, I. (1985) *Urban Rhythms: pop music and popular culture*, London: Macmillan; New York: St Martin's Press.

Chambers, I. and Curti, L. (1982) 'Silent Frontiers: an Italian debate on the "crisis of reason"', *Screen Education*, 41.

Chapple, S. and Garofalo, R. (1977) *Rock'n' Roll Is Here To Pay*, Chicago: Nelson-Hall.

Clarke, J. (1979) 'Capital and culture: the post-war working class revisited' in Clarke, J., Critcher, C. and Johnson, R. (eds) (1979).

Clarke, J., Critcher, C. and Johnson, R. (eds) (1979) *Working Class Culture. Studies in history and theory*, London: Hutchinson.

Cohen, P. (1985) 'Towards Youthopia', *Marxism Today*, October.

Colin, S. (1977) *And The Bands Played On*, London: Elm Tree/Hamish Hamilton.

Colls, R. and Dodd, P. (1985) 'Representing the Nation – British Documentary Film, 1930–45', *Screen*, vol. 26: 1.

Core, P. (1984) *Camp: The lie that tells the truth*, London: Plexus.

Coward, R. (1984) *Female Desire*, London: Paladin.

Cummings, T. (1975) 'Gloria Gaynor and the Disco Boom', *Black Music*, June.

Cunningham, H. (1980) *Leisure in the Industrial Revolution*, London: Croom Helm.

Curran, J. and Porter, V. (eds) (1983) *British Cinema History*, London: Weidenfeld and Nicolson.

Debord, G. (1970) *The Society of the Spectacle*, Chicago: Red and Black.

Deleuze, G. (1969) *Logique du Sens*, Paris: Minuit.

Del Sapio, M. (forthcoming) 'Effetti di superfice: giochi di manipolazione nell'archivio degli stili', *Anglistica*.

Derbyshire, P. (1983) 'George is dead. Boys from the Blackstuff: A British TV drama', *ZG*, 10.

Dickens, C. (1911) *Dombey and Son*, 2 vols, London: Chapman & Hall.

Dyer, R. (1973) *Light Entertainment*, London: British Film Institute.

—— (1979a) *Stars*, London: British Film Institute.

—— (1979b) 'In Defence of Disco', *Gay Left*, 8.

—— (1985) 'A Passage to India', *Marxism Today*, April.

Dyer, R., Geraghty, C., Jordan, M., Lovell, T., Paterson, R. and Stewart, J. (1981) *Coronation Street*, London: British Film Institute.

Eagleton, T. (1983) *Literary Theory*, Oxford: Blackwell.

Elsaesser, T. (1981) 'Narrative Cinema and Audience-Oriented Aesthetics' in Bennett, T., Boyd-Bowman, S., Mercer, C. and Wollacott, J. (eds) (1981).

Esher, L. (1983) *A Broken Wave: The Rebuilding of England 1940–1980*, Harmondsworth: Penguin.

Farr, M. (1964) 'Design' in Thompson, D. (ed.) (1964).

Feuer, J. (1982) *The Hollywood Musical*, Indiana: Indiana University Press.

Fiske, J. and Hartley, J. (1978) *Reading Television*, London and New York: Methuen.

Fiske, J. and Watts, J. (1985) 'Video Games: Inverted Pleasures', *Australian Journal of Cultural Studies*, 3:1.

Fleming, D. and Muirden, A. (1985) 'Notes from Practice', *The Media Education Journal*, 3.

Foss, P. (1984) 'Despero Ergo Sum' in Frankovits (ed.) (1984).

Foster, H. (1985) *Postmodern Culture*, London: Pluto.

Foucault, M. (1979) *Discipline and Punish*, Harmondsworth: Penguin.

Frankovits, A. (ed.) (1984) *Seduced and Abandoned, The Baudrillard Scene*, Glebe: Stonemoss Services.

Frith, S. (1978) *The Sociology of Rock*, London: Constable.

—— (1981) ' "The magic that can set you free": The ideology of Folk and the myth of the Rock Community', *Popular Music*, 1, Cambridge: Cambridge University Press.

—— (1983) 'The Pleasures of the Heath', *Formations of Pleasure*, London: Routledge & Kegan Paul.

Gargani, A. (ed.) (1979) *Crisi della ragione*, Turin: Einaudi.

Graham, D. (1981) 'The End of Liberalism', *ZG*, 2.

Gramsci, A. (1971) *Selections from the Prison Notebooks*, London: Lawrence and Wishart.

Hall, S. (1972) 'The Social Eye of Picture Post', *Working Papers in Cultural Studies*, 2, Centre for Contemporary Cultural Studies, Birmingham.

—— (1977) 'The Hinterland of Science: Ideology and the "Sociology of Knowledge" ' in Centre for Contemporary Cultural Studies (1978).

—— (1980) 'Cultural Studies and the Centre: some problematics and problems' in Hall, S., Hobson, D., Lowe, A. and Willis, P. (eds) (1980).

Hall, S., Critcher, C., Jefferson, T., Clarke, J. and Roberts, B. (1978) *Policing the Crisis: Mugging, the State, and Law and Order*, London: Macmillan.

Hall, S., Hobson, D., Lowe, A. and Willis, P. (eds) (1980) *Culture, Media, Language*, London: Hutchinson.

Hall, S. and Jefferson, T. (eds) (1976) *Resistance through Rituals: Youth subcultures in post-war Britain*, London: Hutchinson.

Hall, S. and Whannell, P. (1964) *The Popular Arts*, London: Hutchinson.

Haralambos, M. (1974) *Right On: From Blues to Soul in Black America*, London: Eddison.

Harper, S. (1983) 'Art Direction and Costume Design' in Aspinall, S. and Murphy, R. (eds) (1983).

Hatton, B. (1985) 'Who is Sylvia? What is NATO?', *ZG*, 13.

Hebdige, D. (1979) *Subculture: The Meaning of Style*, London and New York: Methuen.

—— (1981) 'Towards a cartography of taste 1935–1962', *Block*, 4; reprinted in an abridged form in Waites, B., Bennett, T. and Martin, G. (eds) (1982).

—— (1981) 'Object as image: the Italian scooter cycle', *Block*, 5.

—— (1982) 'Hiding in the light', *Ten.8*, 9.

—— (1983) 'In poor taste. Notes on pop', *Block*, 8.

—— (1985) 'The bottom line on Planet One', *Ten.8*, 19.

Higson, A. (1983) 'Critical Theory and British Cinema', *Screen*, vol. 24: 4–5.

Hill, J. (1983) 'Working Class Realism and Sexual Reaction: Some Theses on the British "New Wave" ' in Curran, J. and Porter, V. (eds) (1983).

Hobsbawm, E. (1969) *Industry and Empire*, Harmondsworth: Penguin.

Hobson, D. (1982) *Crossroads: The Drama of a Soap Opera*, London: Methuen.

Hoggart, R. (1958) *The Uses of Literacy*, Harmondsworth: Penguin.

Hood, S. (1983) 'The Documentary Film Movement' in Curran, J. and Porter, V. (eds) (1983).

Hosokawa, S. (1984) 'The Walkman effect', *Popular Music*, 4, Cambridge: Cambridge University Press.

Humphries, S. (1981) *Hooligans or Rebels*, Oxford: Basil Blackwell.

Hunt, A. (1964) 'The Film' in Thompson, D. (ed.) (1964).

Hustwitt, M. (1983) 'The emergence of the record industry in Britain, 1898 to 1932', paper delivered at the University of Kent.

Jameson, F. (1984) 'Post Modernism or the Cultural Logic of late Capitalism', *New Left Review*, 144.

Jones, L. (1963) *Blues People*, New York: Morrow.

Kaplan, E. A. (ed.) (1980) *Women in Film Noir*, London: British Film Institute.

Kerouac, J. (1958) *On the Road*, London: Deutsch.

Laclau, E. (1986) 'Metaphor and Social Antagonisms', in Nelson, C. and Grossberg, L. (eds) (1986).

Latimer, D. (1984) 'Jameson and Post-Modernism', *New Left Review*, 148.

Lee, E. (1982) *Folk Song and Music Hall*, London: Routledge & Kegan Paul.

Lipman, A. (1985) 'The world of SALVADOR DISNEY', *City Limits*, 190.

Lippard, L. (ed.) (1966) *Pop Art*, London: Thames & Hudson.

Lloyd, A. L. (1975) *Folk Song in England*, London: Paladin.

Lyotard, J.-F. (1984) *The Postmodern Condition: A Report on Knowledge*, Manchester: Manchester University Press.

MacCabe, C. (1981) 'Realism and Cinema: Notes on some Brechtian Theses' in Bennett, T., Boyd-Bowman, S., Mercer, C. and Wollacott, J. (eds) (1981).

MacInnes, C. (1961) *Absolute Beginners*, London: MacGibbon & Kee.

—— (1969) *Sweet Saturday Night*, London: Panther.

McRobbie, A. (1980) 'Settling Accounts with Subcultures', *Screen Education*, 34.

Mailer, N. (1957) 'The White Negro' in *Advertisements for Myself*, London: Panther.

Medhurst, A. (1985) 'Can Chaps Be Pin-Ups?', *Ten.8*, 17.

Melly, G. (1970) *Owning-up*, Harmondsworth: Penguin.

—— (1972) *Revolt into Style*, Harmondsworth: Penguin.

Merton, R. (1968) 'Comment', *New Left Review*, 47.

Minns, R. (1980) *Bombers and Mash*, London: Virago.

Mitchell, J. (1971) *Woman's Estate*, Harmondsworth: Penguin.

Morin, E. (1956) *Le cinéma ou l'homme imaginaire*, Paris: Editions de Minuit.

—— (1962) *L'esprit du temps*, Paris: Grasset.

Mulhern, F. (1979) *The Moment of 'Scrutiny'*, London: New Left Books.

Murphy, R. (1983) 'A Rival to Hollywood? The British Film Industry in the Thirties', *Screen*, vol. 24: 4–5.

Nairn, T. (1981) *The Break-up of Britain*, London: Verso.

Neale, S. (1981) 'Genre and Cinema' in Bennett, T., Boyd-Bowman, S., Mercer, C. and Wollacott, J. (eds) (1981).

Nelson, C. and Grossberg, L. (eds) (1986) *Marxism and the Interpretation of Culture*, Urbana-Champaign: University of Illinois Press.

232

Nevett, T. R. (1982) *Advertising in Britain*, London: Heinemann.

The New Museum of Contemporary Art (1984) *Difference: On Representation and Sexuality*, New York: The New Museum of Contemporary Art.

Norris, C. (1982) *Deconstruction: Theory and Practice*, London and New York: Methuen.

Orwell, G. (1970) *Collected Essays, Journalism and Letters*, 4 volumes, Harmondsworth: Penguin.

Palmer, T. (1977) *All You Need is Love*, London: Futura.

Paz, O. (1967) *The Labyrinth of Solitude*, London: Allen Lane.

Pearson, G. (1983) *Hooligan*, London: Macmillan.

Perry, G. (1975) *The Great British Picture Show*, London: Paladin.

Place, J. (1980) 'Women in film noir' in Kaplan E. A. (ed.) (1980).

Priestley, J. B. (1968) *Angel Pavement*, Harmondsworth: Penguin.

Pryce, K. (1979) *Endless Pressure*, Harmondsworth: Penguin.

Punter, D. (1980) *The Literature of Terror*, London and New York: Longman.

Rambali, P. (1984) 'The hip hop won't stop', *The Face*, 49.

Reid, D. A. (1982) 'Interpreting the Festival Calendar: Wakes and Fairs as Carnivals' in Storch, R. D. (ed.) (1982).

Rella, F. (1984) *Metamorfosi*, Milan: Feltrinelli.

Roberts, R. (1973) *The Classic Slum*, Harmondsworth: Penguin.

Russell, J. and Gablik, S. (eds) (1969) *Pop Art Redefined*, London: Thames & Hudson.

Scharf, A. (1975) *Art and Photography*, Harmondsworth: Penguin.

Shepherd, J. (1982) *Tin Pan Alley*, London: Routledge & Kegan Paul.

Smith, A. C., Blackwell, T. and Immirzi, E. (1975) *Paper Voices*, London: Chatto & Windus.

Sontag, S. (1979a) *On Photography*, Harmondsworth: Penguin.

—— (1979b) 'Notes on Camp' in *A Susan Sontag Reader*, Harmondsworth: Penguin.

Stack, O. (1969) *Pasolini On Pasolini*, London: Thames & Hudson/BFI.

Stedman-Jones, G. (1982) 'Working-class culture and working-class politics in London, 1870–1900: Notes on the remaking of a working class' in Waites, B., Bennett, T. and Martin, G. (eds) (1982).

Steward, S. and Garratt, S. (1984) *Signed Sealed and Delivered: True Life Stories of Women in Pop*, London: Pluto; Boston: South End Press.

Storch, R. D. (ed.) (1982) *Popular Culture and Custom in Nineteenth-Century England*, London: Croom Helm.

Tasker, P. (1982) 'Over the points and off the rails: Pop music and British TV', *Primetime*, vol. 1: 4.

Thompson, D. (ed.) (1964) *Discrimination and Popular Culture*, Harmondsworth: Penguin.

Thompson, E. P. (1968) *The Making of the English Working Class*, Harmondsworth: Penguin.

Tickner, L. (1984) 'Sexuality and/in Representation' in The New

Museum of Contemporary Art (1984).

Toop, D. (1984) *The Rap Attack: African Jive to New York Hip Hop*, London: Pluto; Boston: South End Press.

Tosches, N. (1985) *Country*, New York: Scribner.

Vattimo, G. and Rovatti, P. A. (eds) (1983) *Il pensiero debole*, Milan: Feltrinelli.

Virilio, P. and Lotringer, S. (1983) *Pure War*, New York: Semiotext(e).

Vulliamy, G. and Lee, E. (1982) *Popular Music: A Teacher's Guide*, London: Routledge & Kegan Paul.

Waites, B., Bennett, T. and Martin, G. (eds) (1982) *Popular Culture: past and present*, London: Croom Helm.

Walvin, J. (1978) *Leisure and Society, 1830–1950*, London: Longman.

Warpole, K. (1983) *Dockers and Detectives*, London: Verso.

Warshow, R. (1962) 'The Gangster as Tragic Hero' in *The Immediate Experience*, New York: Doubleday.

Waugh, E. (1951) *Brideshead Revisited*, Harmondsworth: Penguin.

Weiner, M. J. (1985) *English Culture and the Decline of the Industrial Spirit, 1850–1980*, Harmondsworth: Penguin.

Widdowson, P. (ed.) (1982) *Re-Reading English*, London and New York: Methuen.

Williams, R. (1958) *Culture and Society 1780–1950*, London: Chatto & Windus.

—— (1961) *The Long Revolution*, London: Chatto & Windus.

—— (1973) *The Country and the City*, London: Chatto & Windus.

—— (1974) *Television. Technology and Cultural Form*, London: Fontana.

—— (1977) *Marxism and Literature*, Oxford: Oxford University Press.

—— (1980) *Problems in Materialism and Culture*, London: Verso.

Willis, P. (1977) *Learning to Labour*, Farnborough: Saxon House.

Winship, J. (1981) 'Woman becomes an "Individual" – Femininity and Consumption in Women's Magazines, 1954–69', *Stencilled Occasional Paper*, 65, Centre for Contemporary Cultural Studies, Birmingham.

Wolfe, T. (1966) *The Kandy-Kolored Tangerine Flake Streamline Baby*, London: Cape.

X, M. (1968) *The Autobiography of Malcolm X*, Harmondsworth: Penguin.

York, P. (1984) *Modern Times*, London: Heinemann.

INDEX

239

242